MAN'S CLUB

POPOVERS
to Panache

Food with a Flair from The Village Club

POPOVERS
to Panache

Food with a Flair from The Village Club

*The Village Club was founded in 1956 to serve the community through social, educational and philanthropic activities.
A portion of the proceeds from the sale of this cookbook will be returned to the community through
The Village Woman's Club Foundation, the philanthropic arm of the club.*

Published by The Village Club
190 East Long Lake Road
Bloomfield Hills, Michigan 48304
248-644-3450
www.thevillageclub.org

© 2006 by The Village Club of Bloomfield Hills, Michigan
Photographs on the cover and pages 1, 11, 29, 47, 65, 83, and 135 © by Yakov Faytlin
Photograph on page 117 © by Martha Quay

This cookbook is a collection of favorite recipes, which are not necessarily original recipes.
Each recipe has been tested and tasted by a panel of experienced cooks from The Village Club.

Library of Congress Control Number: 2006923903
ISBN: 0-9773559-0-X

Edited, Designed and Manufactured by
Favorite Recipes® Press

P.O. Box 305142
Nashville, Tennessee 37230
800-358-0560

Art Director: Steve Newman
Book Design: Sheri Ferguson
Project Editor: Linda Bennie

Printed by Shenzhen Donnelley Printing Co., Ltd, China subsidiary of RR Donnelley, Chicago, Illinois, U.S.A.
First Printing 2006   7,500 Copies

*The setting on the front cover was designed and the accessories were selected by Jon Gerych of
Gerych's Graziella LTD, Birmingham, Michigan, and photographed by Yakov Faytlin in The Village Club library.*

Contents

4   About The Village Club

5   About the Book

6   The Village Woman's Club Foundation

7   Cookbook Development Committee

7   Recipe Collectors, Testers, and Tasters

8   Many, Many Thanks

9   More Thanks

9   Sidebar Art

10   APPETIZERS

28   SOUPS

46   SALADS

64   BRUNCH

82   ENTREES

116   SIDE DISHES

134   DESSERTS

169   Recipe Contributors

171   Index

175   Order Information

ABOUT THE VILLAGE CLUB

Welcome to The Village Club—a city club located in the lovely, wooded, rolling landscape of Bloomfield Hills, Michigan. The natural beauty of this area, with its winding roads, tranquil lakes, and narrow curving streets, adds to the country-like flavor and provides an attractive residential setting.

The Village Club provides a unique, private club experience and a gracious friendly environment for its members, while offering fine dining and cultural, educational, social, and philanthropic opportunities. The Club offers professionally led educational classes and lectures on a wide variety of topics, including cooking, gardening, finances, current events, history, religion, music, dance, exercise, antiques, architecture, creative art, photography, and bridge. All classes are open to the public. Special events include cultural activities and travel. Social events take place each month.

The Village Woman's Club Foundation is the philanthropic arm of the Club. We are proud of our annual grants to educational, cultural, and human service organizations in the tri-county area. Since its incorporation in 1983, The Village Woman's Club Foundation has given more than one million dollars to area organizations.

ABOUT THE BOOK

We hope the vintage and current photographs throughout this book capture the flavor of The Village Club's past and present. Beautiful table settings, styled by prominent area merchants, include lovely floral arrangements that have become a beloved Club tradition. The Village Club is special in so many ways, including the number of talented cooks as evidenced by the more than 500 favorite recipes received by the Cookbook Committee. Each recipe was tested and tasted. Although most were judged good to outstanding, we did not have space for all of them. In this book we present to you "the best of the best."

We have included favorite traditional recipes served in our dining room, as well as recipes from our first two cookbooks, *Food With A Flair* (1971) and *Food With A Flair II* (1981). You will notice differences from then to now. Over time our tastes have changed and our cooking reflects a new direction. We have become more aware of fresh and natural foods free of additives and preservatives. We've incorporated sun-dried tomatoes, goat cheese, pine nuts, salsas, and a variety of vinegars and flavored oils. We have shifted from formal meals to more simple, but well-planned meals. Today we want easy-to-read recipes, fresh ingredients, and a minimum of fuss. And that is what we have tried to bring to you in *Popovers to Panache: Food with a Flair from The Village Club*. This third cookbook published by The Village Club commemorates our 50th anniversary and is titled after the Club's signature popovers.

So… enjoy! Some recipes are old, some new, some familiar, others unusual, some easy to prepare, and many quite elegant. You will find that some are fabulous, some refreshing, and some quite aromatic. We hope that *Popovers to Panache* brings you "the best you've ever had"… the proof will be in the eating.

Bon Appétit!

THE VILLAGE WOMAN'S CLUB FOUNDATION

The Village Woman's Club Foundation takes pride in promoting philanthropy in the form of grants that further educational, cultural, and human services in the Oakland, Wayne, Macomb tri-county area of Michigan. A portion of the sales of this book will be returned to the community through the Foundation. Grants to area organizations have totaled over one million dollars since the Foundation was established in 1983. Some of the agencies receiving grants in recent years include the following:

Alternatives for Girls

Assistance League of Southeastern Michigan

Baldwin Church and Center

Big Brothers—Big Sisters

BASCC (Birmingham Area Seniors Coordinating Council)

Birmingham Bloomfield Families in Action

Birmingham Youth Assistance Committee

Bloomfield SCAMP

Bloomfield Youth Guidance

Bound Together

Boys and Girls Clubs of Southeastern Michigan

Boy Scouts—Clinton Valley/Detroit

Cabrini Clinic

Cass Community Social Services

Cass Corridor Youth Advocates

Child Abuse and Neglect Council

Christ Child House

Common Ground Sanctuary

The Community House

Cornerstone Schools

Cranbrook Peace Foundation

Crossroads for Youth

Crossroads of Michigan

Detroit Institute for Children

Eton Academy

FAR Conservatory

Fort Street Open Door

Furniture Bank/Oakland County

Gilda's Club

Girl Scouts of Macomb

HAVEN

Horizon's Upward Bound

Hospice of Michigan

Jesuit Volunteer Corps

Judson Center

Lighthouse PATH

Lourdes, Inc.

Maplegrove (Henry Ford Health System)

Meadowbrook Performing Arts

Methodist Children's Home

Michigan Opera Theatre

New Horizons Rehab Services

Oakland Family Services

Open Hands Food Pantry

Penrickton Center for Blind Children

Pewabic Pottery

Plowshares Theatre

Pontiac Osteopathic Hospital— Children's Clinic

Providence Food Pantry

Readings for the Blind

Recordings for the Blind/Dyslexic

Sharing and Caring/ William Beaumont Hospital

St. Patrick's Senior Center

Student Mentor Program

TimRo

Wolverine Human Services

Women's Survival Center Oakland

COOKBOOK DEVELOPMENT COMMITTEE

Creating this cookbook has been a great experience for everyone involved, and one that would have been impossible without the dedication, commitment, and total support of the cookbook committee, each of whom made essential contributions:

Linda Wilson, Chairman	Anne Farnen, Non-Recipe Text	Eunice Raar, Recipe Testing
Barbara Ballantyne, Recipe Testing	Jeanette Keramedjian, PR/Marketing	Louise Simpson, Historian
Camille Breen, Non-Recipe Text	Denise McKewan, Recipe Collection	Anita Terry, Recipe Collection
Dorothy Ellis, Non-Recipe Text	Nancy Peil, Layout and Design	

The Recipe Collection Committee gathered and categorized more than 500 recipes submitted by Village Club members.

The Recipe Testing Committee tested every recipe submitted. Cookbook committee members and a special group of dedicated volunteers faithfully "reported for duty" each Thursday to prepare and taste recipes. It was informative, fun, and fattening.

The Layout and Design Chairman was responsible for the design coordination, which required developing plans, selecting the photographer and sponsors, and finalizing selection of photographs. Assisting were Mary Smart, Nancy Spence, and Pat Wasson.

The Village Club Historian and the Non-Recipe Text Committee gathered historical photographs and information about our Club and community, researched cooking tips, techniques, and hints to clarify recipe instructions, and wrote the descriptive text.

Our Public Relations and Marketing Director used her considerable skill to help us determine and reach our full audience and goals.

Most important, regular meetings were presided over by our dedicated chairman, Linda Wilson, who kept us moving forward and served as liaison between the committees, the book's manufacturer, and The Village Club Board of Directors.

RECIPE COLLECTORS, TESTERS, AND TASTERS

The following individuals participated in the collection, testing, and tasting of the recipes. We are most appreciative of those who worked so hard to make sure that every recipe in this book is perfect.

Barbara Ballantyne	Dorothy Ellis	Jeanne Hackett	Nancy Peil	Louise Simpson
Martha Beechler	Anne Farnen	Pat Haupt	Eunice Raar	Barbara Sobey
Camille Breen	Gwen Forbes	Nancy Kleckner	Mary Ann Rosenberger	Sally Struck
Sharrie Cheff	Mickie Frederick	Chris Lamarche	Barbara Russell	Anita Terry
Phyllis Clark	Peggy Freeman	Sue Leydorf	Jean Schuler	Linda Wilson
Karen DeKoker	Judy Gardner	Denise McKewan	Kathy Shaieb	

Many, Many Thanks

We are very grateful to our talented photographer, who provided the beautiful color photographs
of settings in special rooms of The Village Club.

Yakov Faytlin Photography

Birmingham, Michigan

The following area merchants designed the settings and selected the lovely
objects to be included in the color photographs.

Festivities

Mary Beth, Doug, Diana and Rob Winkworth

Birmingham, Michigan

La Belle Provence

Leslie Benser and Liz Fallert

Birmingham, Michigan

The Fuchsia Frog

Birmingham, Michigan

Studio 330

Randy Forester

Bloomfield Hills, Michigan

Gerych's Graziella LTD

Jon Gerych

Birmingham, Michigan

Veranda

Martha Quay and Jane James

Bloomfield Hills, Michigan

The Italian Dish

Holly Anselmi

Birmingham, Michigan

Woodward & Maple

Dulce Fuller

Birmingham, Michigan

The wine suggestions paired with selected recipes were researched and written by:

Bill Schwab

Sommelier at Papa Joe's Gourmet Market

Birmingham, Michigan

More Thanks

The following individuals and organizations contributed significantly to this project, and their extraordinary efforts are greatly appreciated.

The Village Club Staff Members
Support of Volunteers in Recipe Collection and
Preparation of the Grounds and Building for Photographs

Gary Hendrickson
Village Club Staff Member
Computer Expertise on Vintage Photographs

The Village Club Chef Chris Richter and Staff
Recipes for Traditional Dining Room Favorites

Seegerpeople Photo Studio
Nan Wattles, Birmingham, Michigan

Allied Printing
Barbara Murphy
Ferndale, Michigan

Blossoms
Dale Morgan, Birmingham, Michigan

Smith and Hawkins
Rochester Hills, Michigan

Sidebar Art

*The sidebar art shown throughout this book is a detail of the low-relief plaster ceiling in
The Village Club library showing strapwork and design elements relating to the British tradition of the arts.*

Crab Meat and Shrimp Cocktail
  with Red Pepper Aïoli 13
Snack-Style Shrimp 14
Prosciutto and Ricotta Pita Pockets 15
Lemon Parmesan Artichoke Bottoms 15
Mushroom Roll-Ups 16
Olive Paste and Blue Cheese Canapés 16
Snow Peas Stuffed with Herb Cheese 17
Walnut- and Cheese-Stuffed Cucumbers . .17
Apricot Coins .18
Smoked Salmon Spread 19
Smoked Trout and Shrimp Pâté 19
Basil and Currant Spread 20

Curried Mélange Cheese Spread 20
Apple-Topped Brie 21
Brie with Apricots and
  Pine Nuts 21
Mediterranean Cheese Torte 22
Crab and Artichoke Dip 22
Baked Vidalia Onion Dip 23
Reuben Cocktail Dip 24
Roasted Red Pepper Dip 24
White Bean Dip 25
Brandy Slush 25
Pretty Peach Cocktail 26
Cosmopolitan Cocktail 27

APPETIZERS
Appetizers

The setting on the facing page was designed and the accessories were selected by Holly Anselmi, Deb Roz, and Erin Wass of The Italian Dish, Birmingham, Michigan, and photographed by Yakov Faytlin at the foot of the stone steps outside The Village Club dining room.

APPETIZERS

Appetizers

DINING ROOM CIRCA 1961

The beautifully ornate dining room in the Winningham House was once the cow stable of the original barn. The Swedish design fireplace surrounded by walnut veneer walls had been part of a prize-winning exhibit at the New York Museum of Modern Art. Although the dining room has been enlarged several times since 1961, it still has many large windows featuring wonderful views of the beautiful back gardens and patio of The Village Club.

CRAB MEAT AND SHRIMP COCKTAIL WITH RED PEPPER AIOLI

RED PEPPER AIOLI

1 pasteurized egg or equivalent
amount of pasteurized egg substitute
1 teaspoon white wine vinegar
1 large red bell pepper, roasted, peeled
and chopped
1/2 teaspoon chopped garlic
1 tablespoon chopped fresh parsley
1/4 teaspoon salt
Pinch of cayenne pepper
1/2 cup olive oil
1/2 cup vegetable oil

COCKTAIL

2 large Hass avocados, chopped
2 teaspoons fresh lemon juice
2 tablespoons mayonnaise
1 tablespoon chopped green onions
1 tablespoon chopped shallots
2 teaspoons Dijon mustard
Pinch of salt
8 ounces lump crab meat
8 ounces large shrimp, boiled,
peeled and chilled
1/2 cup finely chopped tomatoes

For the aïoli, mix the egg and vinegar in a food processor by pulsing for 10 seconds. Add the roasted bell pepper, garlic, parsley, salt and cayenne pepper and process until mixed. Add the olive oil and vegetable oil gradually, processing constantly until the mixture forms a thick emulsion. Adjust the seasonings. Pour into a container with a tight-fitting lid. Chill, covered, for up to 1 day.

For the cocktail, combine the avocados and 1 teaspoon of the lemon juice in a bowl and toss gently to coat. Chill, covered, for 30 to 60 minutes.

Mix the remaining lemon juice, the mayonnaise, green onions, shallots, Dijon mustard and salt in a large bowl. Fold in the crab meat. Adjust the seasonings. Chill, covered, until serving time. Divide the avocados among four to six martini glasses or individual compotes or bowls. Add a dollop of the aïoli and equal portions of the crab meat mixture to each glass. Arrange the shrimp around the rims of the glasses. Top each cocktail with a heaping tablespoonful of the tomatoes. Garnish with French bread croutons, the remaining aïoli and chives. Serve immediately. *Serves 4 to 6.*

*T*o quickly ripen hard avocados, punch holes in a paper bag and add the avocados and an apple. Close the bag and let stand at room temperature for 2 to 3 days. The apple gives off a gas that makes the avocados ripen more rapidly.

SNACK-STYLE SHRIMP

1¹/2 pounds fresh deveined peeled shrimp
1/2 cup celery tops
3¹/2 teaspoons salt
1/4 cup mixed pickling spices
2 cups sliced onions
7 or 8 bay leaves
1¹/2 cups vegetable oil
3/4 cup white vinegar
1¹/2 teaspoons salt
2¹/2 teaspoons celery seeds
2¹/2 tablespoons capers with liquid
Dash of Tabasco sauce

Place the shrimp in a saucepan of boiling water. Stir in the celery tops, 3^1/2 teaspoons salt and the pickling spices. Cook for 2 to 3 minutes or until the shrimp turn pink. Drain and rinse under cool water. Layer the shrimp, onions and bay leaves in a shallow dish. Combine the oil, vinegar, 1^1/2 teaspoons salt, the celery seeds, capers and Tabasco sauce in a bowl and mix well.

Pour the oil mixture evenly over the shrimp mixture. Chill, covered, for at least 24 hours.

Remove and discard the bay leaves and some of the sauce before serving. *Serves 10 to 12.*

Note: This is an excellent dish to make ahead of time for a party. It's very tasty and will keep for a few days.

Another idea for using bay leaves . . .

Bay leaves will repel troublesome insects that try to invade beans, pasta, flour, and other dried food products. To deter pests, just place a bay leaf in the storage container. Don't worry . . . the bay leaf flavor doesn't mix with your pasta, beans, or other products.

PROSCIUTTO AND RICOTTA PITA POCKETS

4 small pockets pita bread
1/2 cup pistachios
1 tablespoon honey
1 tablespoon olive oil
4 ounces thickly sliced prosciutto
1/2 cup ricotta cheese
1/4 small cantaloupe, peeled and thinly sliced

Cut each pita into six wedges. Combine the pistachios, honey and olive oil in a food processor and process until the pistachios are finely chopped. Spread equal portions of the pistachio mixture inside each pita wedge and add equal portions of the prosciutto.

Place the stuffed wedges on a nonstick baking sheet. Bake at 375 degrees for 10 minutes or until heated through and crisp. Remove to a serving plate and top the wedges with equal portions of ricotta cheese and cantaloupe. Garnish with fresh thyme. *Serves 24.*

LEMON PARMESAN ARTICHOKE BOTTOMS

2 (14-ounce) cans artichoke bottoms, drained,
rinsed and patted dry
1 1/2 cups (6 ounces) grated Parmesan cheese
1/2 cup regular or reduced-calorie mayonnaise
3 large garlic cloves, finely chopped
1 teaspoon grated lemon zest
2 teaspoons fresh lemon juice
Salt and pepper to taste
1/4 cup pine nuts

Place the artichokes rounded sides down in a lightly greased 8×8-inch baking dish. Combine the cheese, mayonnaise, garlic, lemon zest, lemon juice, salt and pepper in a bowl and mix well.

Mound equal portions of the cheese mixture over the artichokes. Sprinkle with the pine nuts. Bake at 375 degrees for 20 minutes or until heated through. Garnish with chopped fresh parsley. *Serves 14 to 16.*

MUSHROOM ROLL-UPS

3 ounces cream cheese, softened
3 ounces fresh mushrooms, finely chopped
1 tablespoon milk or cream
1/4 teaspoon seasoned salt
1 (8-count) can refrigerator crescent rolls
1 egg white
Sesame seeds

Combine the cream cheese, mushrooms, milk and seasoned salt in a bowl and mix well. Unroll the crescent roll dough on a work surface. Separate into four rectangles, pressing the perforations to seal. Spread equal portions of the mushroom mixture over the rectangles.

Roll up and pinch the seams to seal. Brush with the egg white and coat with sesame seeds.

Cut each log into 1 1/2-inch slices and arrange on a nonstick baking sheet. Bake at 400 degrees for 10 minutes. *Serves 24.*

OLIVE PASTE AND BLUE CHEESE CANAPES

4 ounces pitted cured black olives
1 large garlic clove, pressed
2 tablespoons pine nuts, toasted
3 tablespoons olive oil
1 baguette, cut into 1/4-inch slices
4 to 8 ounces blue cheese, Roquefort cheese or
Gorgonzola cheese, crumbled

Combine the olives, garlic, pine nuts and olive oil in a food processor and process until finely chopped. Spread equal portions of the olive mixture over each bread slice.

Top each canapé with a small amount of the blue cheese. Garnish each with a slice of black olive. *Serves 24.*

SNOW PEAS STUFFED WITH HERB CHEESE

25 medium-large snow peas
6 ounces cream cheese, softened
3 scallions (white part only), chopped
1 garlic clove, finely chopped
1/2 cup mixture of finely chopped fresh basil, dill and parsley

Cook the snow peas in a saucepan of boiling water for 45 seconds. Drain and rinse. Place in ice water for 1 minute. Drain well and dry on paper towels. Split the curved seam of the snow peas using a small sharp knife.

Combine the cream cheese, scallions, garlic and herb mixture in a bowl and mix well.

Spoon the mixture into a pastry bag and pipe a small amount into each snow pea. *Serves 25.*

WALNUT- AND CHEESE-STUFFED CUCUMBERS

8 ounces cream cheese, softened
3 ounces blue cheese
1 tablespoon dry sherry
2 tablespoons finely chopped fresh parsley
1/2 teaspoon garlic powder
1/2 cup chopped walnuts
3 cucumbers (about 8 inches long)

Combine the cream cheese and blue cheese in a food processor and process to mix well. Add the sherry, parsley and garlic powder and process to mix well. Remove to a bowl and stir in the walnuts. Chill, covered, overnight. Rinse the cucumbers and cut into 1-inch slices. Remove the seeds from the center of each slice.

Spoon equal portions of the cheese mixture into the center of each slice. Garnish with parsley sprigs. *Serves 24.*

Note: The cucumbers may be peeled, unpeeled or partially peeled in a decorative pattern. You may use English cucumbers sliced 3/4 inch thick instead of regular cucumbers.

APRICOT COINS

CANDIED WALNUTS
1/4 cup confectioners' sugar
1/8 teaspoon cayenne pepper
1/8 teaspoon salt
4 ounces (about 1 cup) walnut halves

COINS
40 dried apricots (about 6 ounces), preferably Turkish
Water or brandy
4 ounces fresh goat cheese
2 teaspoons milk
2 teaspoons honey
1 tablespoon finely chopped fresh thyme, or
1 1/2 teaspoons dried thyme

For the walnuts, mix the confectioners' sugar, cayenne pepper and salt in a bowl. Cook the walnuts in a saucepan of boiling water for 3 minutes. Drain well and coat immediately with the confectioners' sugar mixture. Place the walnuts on a nonstick baking sheet. Bake at 350 degrees for 10 minutes or until deep golden brown, stirring occasionally. Do not allow the sugar coating to burn. Remove to a wire rack and cool completely.

For the coins, soak the dried apricots in water in a bowl until softened; drain. Combine the goat cheese and milk in a bowl. Beat with an electric mixer for 5 minutes or until smooth and creamy. Spread 1/8 teaspoon of the cheese mixture over each apricot. Drizzle each apricot with a small amount of the honey and sprinkle with thyme. Place one walnut half on top of each apricot and arrange on a serving platter. *Serves 20.*

A simple, yet successful, presentation of fresh fruit, cheeses, and nuts works equally as well before dinner or as a finishing touch after dinner. Some combinations you might try are: Roquefort cheese, sliced Granny Smith apples, and walnuts; Jarlsberg cheese, purple grapes, and cashews; and Brie cheese, figs, and pecans.

SMOKED SALMON SPREAD

8 ounces cream cheese, softened
1 (8-ounce) can red sockeye salmon
$1/4$ cup grated onion
1 teaspoon horseradish
$1/2$ teaspoon salt
$1/2$ teaspoon liquid smoke

Mix the cream cheese, salmon, onion, horseradish, salt and liquid smoke in a bowl.

Spoon into a serving dish. Chill, covered, for several hours. Serve with crackers. *Serves 8.*

SMOKED TROUT AND SHRIMP PATE

12 ounces smoked trout, coarsely chopped
12 ounces cooked bay shrimp, peeled
12 ounces cream cheese, softened
$3/4$ cup chopped chives
3 tablespoons drained capers
1 tablespoon grated lemon zest
Salt and pepper to taste
Small pumpernickel bread slices, baguette slices
or water crackers

Combine the trout and shrimp in a food processor and process until finely chopped. Add the cream cheese and process to mix well. Remove to a bowl.

Stir in the chives, capers, lemon zest, salt and pepper. Remove to a serving dish and place on a platter. Surround with bread slices. *Serves 24 to 36.*

BASIL AND CURRANT SPREAD

^{1}/3 cup olive oil
3 tablespoons chopped fresh basil
1 tablespoon finely chopped garlic
16 ounces cream cheese, softened
3 tablespoons chopped fresh parsley
^{2}/3 cup coarsely chopped walnuts
^{2}/3 cup currants

Combine the olive oil, basil and garlic in a bowl and mix well. Add the cream cheese and mix well. Stir in the parsley, walnuts and currants. Chill 2 hours to overnight.

Spoon the spread into a serving dish. Garnish with walnut halves and parsley and serve with water crackers. *Serves 24.*

CURRIED MELANGE CHEESE SPREAD

8 ounces cream cheese, softened
^{1}/2 cup coarsely chopped green onions
^{1}/2 cup bacon bits
^{1}/2 cup salted peanuts
^{1}/2 cup golden raisins
2 teaspoons sour cream
1^1/2 teaspoons curry powder
1 (8-ounce) jar peach chutney or mango chutney

Combine the cream cheese, green onions, bacon bits, peanuts, raisins, sour cream and curry powder in a food processor. Pulse until coarsely chopped and well mixed.

Mound the mixture onto a serving plate. Spread the chutney over the cream cheese mixture. Serve with crackers. *Serves 12.*

APPLE-TOPPED BRIE

1 tart red apple, chopped
$^1/_2$ cup golden raisins
1 cup apple cider
1 (16-ounce) wheel Brie cheese

1 (16-ounce) wheel Brie cheese
2 tablespoons butter, melted
$^1/_2$ cup pecans
Small bunches of grapes or
   sliced red and green apples

For the brie, combine the apple, raisins and cider in a saucepan. Bring to a boil and simmer for 2 minutes; drain well.

Place the cheese in a baking dish and top with the apple mixture. Bake at 350 degrees for 20 to 30 minutes. Serve with crackers. *Serves 8.*

For the variation, place the cheese in an ovenproof serving dish and brush the top with a small amount of the butter. Mix the remaining butter and the pecans in a bowl. Spoon over the cheese. Bake at 350 degrees for 8 to 10 minutes or until the cheese is softened and the pecans are lightly toasted. Arrange the grapes around the cheese and serve with crackers. *Serves 8.*

BRIE WITH APRICOTS AND PINE NUTS

1 (16-ounce) wheel Brie cheese
$1^1/_2$ teaspoons apricot brandy, Cointreau
   or Cognac
$^1/_3$ cup dried apricots, cut into $^1/_4$-inch strips

3 tablespoons golden raisins
3 tablespoons pine nuts
$4^1/_2$ teaspoons apricot brandy, Cointreau
   or Cognac

Remove the top rind of the cheese with a sharp knife. Place the cheese in an ovenproof serving dish. Poke holes in the top of the cheese with a fork. Drizzle $1^1/_2$ teaspoons brandy over the cheese.

Mix the dried apricots, raisins, pine nuts and $4^1/_2$ teaspoons brandy in a bowl. Spoon over the cheese. Bake at 350 degrees for 8 to 10 minutes or until the cheese is softened. Serve with crackers or baguette slices. *Serves 8.*

MEDITERRANEAN CHEESE TORTE

PESTO

4 cups firmly packed fresh basil
4 garlic cloves
1/4 cup pine nuts
2 (scant) teaspoons salt
2/3 to 1 cup olive oil
1 cup (4 ounces) grated Parmesan cheese

TORTE

1/4 cup extra-light olive oil
2 cups oil-pack sun-dried tomatoes
16 ounces cream cheese, softened
1/3 cup milk

For the pesto, pulse the basil, garlic, pine nuts, salt and olive oil in a food processor just until the basil, garlic and pine nuts are chopped. Add the cheese and process until incorporated. You may reduce the amount of olive oil and process 1/4 cup butter into the mixture until incorporated.

For the torte, coat a decorative mold with 1/4 cup olive oil. Rinse the sun-dried tomatoes with hot water; drain and pat dry. Chop the sun-dried tomatoes. Place the cream cheese in a mixing bowl.

Add the milk gradually, beating constantly until of a spreadable consistency. Spread half the sun-dried tomatoes over the bottom of the mold. Layer with half the pesto and half the cream cheese mixture, spreading to the edge. Repeat the layers with the remaining sun-dried tomatoes, pesto and cream cheese mixture. Chill, covered, for at least 2 hours. Dip the mold into warm water and loosen the side. Unmold onto a serving plate. Bring to room temperature before serving. Garnish with additional sun-dried tomatoes and serve with assorted crackers. *Serves 15.*

CRAB AND ARTICHOKE DIP

4 to 6 pickled jalapeño chiles
16 ounces cream cheese
1/2 cup pickled jalapeño chile liquid
1 (14-ounce) can water-pack artichoke hearts, drained and chopped

1 cup sour cream
16 ounces jumbo lump crab meat, or
 3 (6-ounce) cans crab meat, drained
1/2 cup (2 ounces) grated Parmesan cheese
Salt and white pepper to taste

Cut the jalapeños into thin slices. Combine the cream cheese, jalapeños and jalapeño liquid in a heavy saucepan over low heat. Cook until the cream cheese is melted, stirring occasionally. Stir in the artichoke hearts and sour cream.

Cook until the mixture is heated through. Stir in the crab meat, Parmesan cheese, salt and white pepper. Bring to a simmer, stirring constantly; do not boil. Spoon into a chafing dish and place over a burner or candle. Serve with crackers or toasted pita chips. *Serves 18 to 20.*

BAKED VIDALIA ONION DIP

2 cups (8 ounces) shredded Swiss cheese
1 (8-ounce) can water chestnuts, drained and chopped
2 cups mayonnaise
1/4 cup dry white wine
1 garlic clove, chopped
1/2 teaspoon hot red pepper sauce
2 tablespoons butter
3 large Vidalia onions or other sweet onions, chopped

Combine the cheese, water chestnuts, mayonnaise, wine, garlic and hot sauce in a bowl and mix well. Melt the butter in a skillet over medium heat. Add the onions and sauté for 10 minutes or until tender. Stir into the cheese mixture. Spoon into a lightly greased 2-quart baking dish. Bake at 375 degrees for 25 minutes.

Let stand for 10 minutes before serving. Serve with tortilla chips or crackers. **Serves 24.**

Note: You can lighten this recipe by using nonstick cooking spray instead of butter and using low-fat cheese and mayonnaise.

*T*ry lighting a candle before you begin chopping onions. The flame from the candle neutralizes the sulfuric fumes and helps keep your eyes clear and dry.

REUBEN COCKTAIL DIP

16 ounces cream cheese, softened
1/2 cup plain yogurt
3/4 cup (3 ounces) shredded Swiss cheese
1 garlic clove, finely chopped
1/2 cup drained sauerkraut, chopped
8 ounces lean corned beef, finely chopped
1/2 teaspoon spicy seasoned salt

Combine the cream cheese and yogurt in an ovenproof or microwave-safe bowl and mix well. Stir in the Swiss cheese, garlic, sauerkraut, corned beef and seasoned salt. Cook in a 300-degree oven, microwave or in the top of a double boiler until heated through.

Serve with toasted strips of rye or pumpernickel bread or breadsticks. *Serves 16.*

Note: Low-fat cream cheese and nonfat yogurt may be used to lighten this recipe.

ROASTED RED PEPPER DIP

2 garlic cloves
3 red bell peppers, roasted, peeled and seeded
2 teaspoons lemon juice
1/2 teaspoon seasoned salt
1/4 teaspoon sugar
1/4 teaspoon white pepper
Dash of cayenne pepper (optional)
1/3 cup mayonnaise
3 to 4 ounces cream cheese, softened

Pulse the garlic in a food processor until finely chopped. Add the bell peppers, lemon juice, seasoned salt, sugar, white pepper and cayenne pepper.

Pulse just until puréed. Remove to a bowl. Stir in the mayonnaise. Stir in the cream cheese until of the desired consistency. Serve with corn chips or crackers. *Serves 8.*

WHITE BEAN DIP

1 (15-ounce) can cannellini beans,
drained and rinsed
1/4 cup loosely packed flat-leaf parsley
2 tablespoons fresh lemon juice

1 garlic clove
1/2 teaspoon salt
1/4 teaspoon pepper
1/3 cup olive oil

Pulse the beans, parsley, lemon juice, garlic, salt and pepper in a food processor until the beans, parsley and garlic are coarsely chopped.

Add the olive oil gradually, processing constantly until the mixture is creamy. Remove to a bowl and adjust the seasonings. Serve with toasted pita chips. *Serves 8.*

BRANDY SLUSH

7 cups water
2 cups sugar
2 cups boiling water
4 tea bags
1 (12-ounce) can frozen orange juice
concentrate, thawed

1 (12-ounce) can frozen lemonade
concentrate, thawed
1 (750-milliliter) bottle brandy,
vodka or gin
Club soda or sparkling water

Combine 7 cups water and the sugar in a saucepan. Bring to a boil, stirring frequently. Remove from the heat and cool. Pour 2 cups boiling water over the tea bags in a bowl. Remove and discard the tea bags when cool. Combine the sugar water and tea in a large bowl.

Add the orange juice concentrate, lemonade concentrate and brandy to the tea mixture. Pour into a freezer-safe container with a tight-fitting lid. Freeze until slushy. Fill glasses two-thirds full with slush and top with club soda. *Serves 25.*

Toasted Pita Chips

Split pita breads into halves horizontally and cut into wedges. Arrange on a baking sheet, brush with olive oil and sprinkle with dried oregano, salt and pepper. Bake at 400 degrees for 8 minutes. Turn over and bake until crisp and golden brown.

PRETTY PEACH COCKTAIL

$1/2$ cup boiling water
$1/2$ cup sugar
Fresh lime juice
Coarse sugar
$11/2$ cups (6 ounces) fresh raspberries
1 cup spiced rum
1 cup fresh lime juice
3 cups sliced fresh peaches, or
1 (16-ounce) bag frozen peaches
1 cup ice cubes

Combine the boiling water and sugar in a bowl and stir until the sugar is dissolved. Let cool to room temperature.

Dip the rims of eight martini glasses in lime juice and then in coarse sugar to coat. Purée the raspberries with 2 tablespoons of the sugar water in a blender.

Pour equal amounts of the raspberry purée into the prepared glasses. Rinse the blender container and add the rum, $1/2$ cup simple syrup, 1 cup lime juice, the peaches and ice cubes. Process until puréed. Pour the peach mixture carefully on top of the raspberry layer in the glasses. *Serves 8.*

COSMOPOLITAN COCKTAIL

2 tablespoons vodka
4¹/₂ teaspoons Cointreau
2 teaspoons lime juice
4¹/₂ teaspoons cranberry juice cocktail
Ice

Combine the vodka, Cointreau, lime juice, cranberry juice cocktail and ice in a cocktail shaker or container with a tight-fitting lid and shake well.

Strain the vodka mixture into a cocktail glass and garnish with an orange twist. *Serves 1.*

Wine Suggestions for Appetizers

The appetizer course has two duties: to inspire the appetite and to take the edge off hunger so the meal may be relaxed and savored. The wines one serves with appetizers must serve the same purpose.

The food and wine marriages provided here are time-tested and classic. There are no surprises and therefore the meal begins effortlessly, relaxing your guests and (more importantly) yourself.

All the appetizers that have seafood in them will match perfectly with a French Muscadet. From the Loire Valley, the Melon de Bourgogne grape has a vibrant acidity that makes seafood dance on the palate. These wines should be inexpensive ($9 to $15) and somewhere on the label should be displayed the symbol ∼ which stands for Sur Lie, or "on the lees," which adds richness and complexity.

For the cheese-based appetizers, Apremont is one of the best wine choices. From the south of France, near Switzerland, this little gem brings out the best in all cheeses. Apremont is also great with fondue.

The dips and spreads that are not cheese-based scream for Gamey Noir. The classics are the Beaujolais-Villages and a little known Swiss wine called Dole. Try a Dole if you can find it, or try an Oregon Gamey Noir. Jadot, Latour, and Drouhin all produce great Beaujolais from the towns of Morgon, Moulin-a-Vent, and Brouilly (these names will be in big letters on the label).

Lastly, the mushroom dishes will like a meaty red without being too heavy. Cabernet Franc is the answer. Chinon from France or the California Cabernet Franc are inexpensive ($10 to $15). Ironstone has produced a great red wine for at least ten years and shows no sign of stopping.

Oriental Mushroom Soup 31
Chicken with Wild Rice Chowder 32
Hearty Mexican Soup 32
San Diego Tortilla Soup 33
Senate Bean Soup 33
Cabbage Soup 34
Carrot Dill Soup 34
Crème des Carottes de Crécy 35
Cauliflower Soup 35
Boursin Leek Soup 36
Mushroom Barley Soup 36
Red Pepper Soup
    with Sambuca Cream 37

Spinach Bisque 37
Roquefort and Spinach Soup 38
Thai Coconut Squash Soup 38
Zucchini Soup 39
Curried Squash Soup 40
Tomato Basil Soup 40
Consommé 41
Vegetable Bisque 42
Dynamite Vegetable Chowder 43
Quick Summer Minestrone 43
Tuscan Vegetable Soup 44
Chilled Herbed Cucumber Soup 45
Chilled Hungarian Berry Soup 45

SOUPS
Soups

The setting on the facing page was designed and the accessories were selected by Mary Beth, Doug, Diana and Rob Winkworth of Festivities, Birmingham, Michigan, and photographed by Yakov Faytlin on The Village Club lawn.

2

SOUPS

Soups

REAR VIEW OF THE WINNINGHAM HOUSE CIRCA 1961

The start of this house came about in 1919 when Charles Winningham purchased the property, moved a nearby schoolhouse, and joined it to an existing barn. Additions were made, resulting in a lovely and unique home, occupied by the Winningham family until 1961 when The Village Club purchased it. The seven-acre Village Club property is nestled in its own natural beauty of lovely gardens and old trees. The patio and lawn are often used in nice weather for outdoor events such as weddings, receptions, parties, and concerts.

ORIENTAL MUSHROOM SOUP

4 cups fat-free reduced-sodium chicken broth
3 tablespoons reduced-sodium soy sauce
2 teaspoons grated fresh ginger
3 garlic cloves, crushed
3 cups white cabbage wedges
3 cups assorted mushrooms, sliced
1 cup thinly sliced carrots
2 cups shredded cooked chicken breasts
2 cups fresh udon noodles or cooked linguini
1 cup thinly sliced green onions
2 cups shredded or whole baby spinach leaves
1 tablespoon mirin (sweetened rice wine) (optional)
Freshly ground pepper to taste

Combine the broth, soy sauce, ginger, garlic, cabbage, mushrooms, carrots and chicken in a large saucepan. Cover and bring to a boil. Reduce the heat and simmer for 5 minutes or until the mushrooms are tender. Stir in the noodles, green onions and spinach. Simmer for 2 minutes or until the spinach is wilted. Stir in the mirin and pepper. *Serves 6.*

Note: Oyster mushrooms, cremini mushrooms, portobello mushrooms, shiitake mushroom caps and button mushrooms make a good combination in this soup. You may use one package of frozen assorted mushrooms, thawed, instead of fresh mushrooms. These can be purchased at Trader Joe's stores.

Sauté vegetables in butter or oil before adding them to soup. This seals in their flavor and keeps them firm. Give onions a little extra time, as slow cooking brings out their natural sweetness.

CHICKEN WITH WILD RICE CHOWDER

2 ribs celery, sliced
1 small onion, chopped
1 carrot, sliced
1 (48-ounce) can chicken broth
1 chicken breast, cooked and chopped

1 (6-ounce) package Uncle Ben's original flavor
   wild rice with seasonings
3/4 cup evaporated milk
Salt and pepper to taste

Combine the celery, onion, carrot, broth, chicken and rice in a saucepan. Simmer for 1 hour. Remove 2 cups of the soup to a blender and purée.

Return the purée to the soup. Stir in the evaporated milk and season with salt and pepper. Cook until heated through. *Serves 8.*

HEARTY MEXICAN SOUP

1 chicken, cooked, boned and
   cut into bite-size pieces
1 (24-ounce) jar salsa

1 (15-ounce) can Great Northern beans
1 cup (4 ounces) shredded Mexican-style cheese
Terra strips or crispy tortilla strips

Combine the chicken, salsa and beans in a saucepan and mix well. Cook over medium heat until heated through, stirring frequently. Ladle into soup bowls and top with equal portions of the cheese and Terra strips. *Serves 4 to 6.*

Note: Terra strips can be found in the health-food section of the grocery store.

*I*t is simple to remove fat from a soup if you chill it first. The fat will solidify on top and can easily be removed with a spoon.

SAN DIEGO TORTILLA SOUP

2 cups water
2 (14-ounce) cans chicken broth
1 (14-ounce) can crushed or stewed tomatoes
1 (15-ounce) can black beans, drained and rinsed
1 (15-ounce) can pinto beans
1 (16-ounce) can garbanzo beans
1 garlic clove, pressed
1 bay leaf

$^1/4$ teaspoon cumin
$^1/4$ teaspoon crushed red pepper
12 ounces boneless skinless chicken breasts, cooked and chopped or shredded
2 green onions, chopped
2 tablespoons fresh lime juice
2 teaspoons chopped fresh cilantro
Sliced black olives, shredded cheese, chopped avocado, sour cream and tortilla rounds

Combine the water, broth, tomatoes, black beans, pinto beans, garbanzo beans, garlic, bay leaf, cumin and red pepper in a large saucepan and mix well. Bring to a boil and reduce the heat. Simmer for 5 minutes.

Stir in the chicken, green onions, lime juice and cilantro. Cook until heated through. Remove and discard the bay leaf. Ladle into soup bowls and top with olives, cheese, avocado, sour cream and tortillas. *Serves 5 or 6.*

SENATE BEAN SOUP

$2^1/4$ cups navy beans, sorted and rinsed
8 cups water
1 (1$^1/2$-pound) smoked ham bone
1 cup chopped onion
1 cup chopped celery
2 tablespoons unsalted butter

1 teaspoon nutmeg
1 teaspoon oregano
1 teaspoon basil
1 teaspoon salt
$^1/4$ teaspoon pepper

Soak the beans according to the package directions; drain. Combine the beans, 8 cups water and the ham bone in a large saucepan. Simmer, covered, for 1$^1/2$ hours. Remove 1 cup of the beans to a bowl and mash the beans. Return the beans to the soup. Remove the ham bone.

Trim the meat from the bone. Return the meat to the soup. Sauté the onion and celery in the butter in a skillet until tender. Add to the soup and mix well. Stir in the nutmeg, oregano, basil, salt and pepper. Simmer for 20 minutes or until thickened. *Serves 8.*

CABBAGE SOUP

1 green bell pepper, chopped
2 ribs celery, chopped
1 onion, chopped
2 carrots, thinly sliced
2 tablespoons butter
3 tablespoons all-purpose flour
6 cups chicken stock
8 ounces bacon, crisp-cooked and crumbled

1 bay leaf
4 cups coarsely chopped cabbage
2 tablespoons butter
1/2 cup water
3 tablespoons chopped fresh parsley
Coarsely ground pepper to taste
1/2 cup sour cream

Sauté the bell pepper, celery, onion and carrots in 2 tablespoons butter in a large saucepan for 5 minutes or until tender. Remove from the heat. Add the flour gradually, stirring constantly.

Return to the heat and stir in 1 cup of the stock. Stir in the remaining stock gradually. Stir in the bacon and bay leaf. Simmer, covered, for 20 minutes.

Sauté the cabbage in 2 tablespoons butter in a skillet for 5 minutes. Stir in the water and reduce the heat to low. Simmer, covered, for 10 minutes or until the cabbage is tender-crisp. Add to the soup. Stir in the parsley and pepper. Simmer for 5 minutes. Remove and discard the bay leaf. Ladle into soup bowls and top each serving with a dollop of the sour cream. *Serves 6 to 8.*

CARROT DILL SOUP

A favorite recipe from a past president

1 small onion, chopped
2 tablespoons butter
12 ounces sweet potatoes or yams, cooked and peeled
8 ounces baking potatoes, cooked and peeled
2 pounds carrots, sliced and cooked

5 cups chicken broth
1 tablespoon lemon juice
2 tablespoons finely chopped fresh dill weed
1 1/2 teaspoons salt
1/4 teaspoon pepper

Sauté the onion in the butter in a saucepan until tender. Purée the onion, sweet potatoes, baking potatoes and carrots with the broth in three batches in a food processor.

Pour the purée into a saucepan. Simmer, covered, over low heat for 15 minutes, stirring occasionally. Stir in the lemon juice, dill weed, salt and pepper. *Serves 6 to 8.*

CREME DES CAROTTES DE CRECY

1 large onion, chopped
1/4 cup (1/2 stick) butter
2 pounds carrots, sliced
4 cups chicken broth
2 tablespoons dill weed

1/2 teaspoon salt
1/4 teaspoon cayenne pepper
3 drops of lemon juice
2 cups milk

Sauté the onion in the butter in a saucepan until tender. Stir in the carrots and broth. Simmer for 20 to 30 minutes or until the carrots are very tender. Purée the carrot mixture in batches in a blender.

Return the purée to the saucepan. Stir in the dill weed, salt, cayenne pepper and lemon juice. Cook until heated through. Stir in the milk. Cook until heated through; do not boil. Serve hot or chilled. *Serves 6 to 8.*

CAULIFLOWER SOUP

6 cups cooked cauliflower florets
1 1/2 cups rich chicken stock
1 1/2 cups water
1 cup heavy cream
1 cup milk
3/4 cup finely chopped onion
3/4 cup finely chopped celery

3 tablespoons butter
1 tablespoon sesame seeds
3 tablespoons all-purpose flour
1 teaspoon salt
1/2 teaspoon white pepper
1 cup (4 ounces) shredded Cheddar cheese
Crumbled cooked bacon (optional)

Remove 2 cups of the cauliflower and chop. Set aside and keep warm. Purée the remaining 4 cups cauliflower, the stock and water in a blender. Add the cream and milk and process until mixed. Sauté the onion and celery in the butter in a saucepan until tender. Add the sesame seeds and cook for 2 minutes, stirring constantly.

Stir in the flour and cook for 2 minutes, stirring constantly. Add the cauliflower purée gradually, stirring constantly. Stir in the salt and white pepper. Cook until thickened, stirring frequently. Stir in the reserved cauliflower. Stir in the cheese and bacon. Cook until heated through. *Serves 4 or 5.*

BOURSIN LEEK SOUP

4 to 5 leeks
1 pound ground beef
2 onions, chopped
4 cups beef broth
2 (3$^1/_2$-ounce) packages boursin cheese
Salt and pepper to taste

Remove all but 1 inch of the green part of the leeks. Slit the leeks lengthwise in two places and rinse thoroughly to remove all the dirt trapped between the leaf layers. Slice the leeks thinly. Brown the ground beef with the onions in a large saucepan, stirring until the ground beef is crumbly; drain. Stir in the broth and leeks.

Simmer, covered, for 30 minutes or until the leeks are tender. Add the cheese. Simmer until the cheese is melted, stirring constantly. Season with salt and pepper. *Serves 6.*

Note: For a nice addition to this soup, add mushrooms when sautéing the beef.

MUSHROOM BARLEY SOUP

8 ounces fresh mushrooms, chopped
1 cup chopped onion
1 garlic clove, finely chopped
$^1/_4$ cup ($^1/_2$ stick) butter
8 cups chicken broth
3 tablespoons tomato paste
1 teaspoon salt
1 bay leaf

$^1/_2$ cup barley
1$^1/_2$ cups chopped carrots
1$^1/_2$ cups chopped celery with leaves
$^1/_4$ cup chopped fresh parsley (optional)
8 ounces fresh mushrooms, sliced
2 tablespoons butter
$^1/_4$ cup dry sherry or port
2 cups sour cream

Sauté the chopped mushrooms, onion and garlic in $^1/_4$ cup butter in a large saucepan until the onion is tender. Stir in the broth, tomato paste, salt and bay leaf. Bring to a boil. Stir in the barley and reduce the heat. Simmer, covered, for 1 hour. Stir in the carrots, celery and parsley.

Simmer, covered, for 30 minutes or until the carrots are tender and the barley is cooked. Sauté the sliced mushrooms in 2 tablespoons butter in a skillet for 5 minutes. Add to the soup. Stir in the sherry. Remove and discard the bay leaf. Ladle into soup bowls and top each serving with a dollop of the sour cream. *Serves 8.*

RED PEPPER SOUP WITH SAMBUCA CREAM

SOUP

3 tablespoons cottonseed oil
6 red bell peppers, roasted, peeled, seeded and chopped
2 onions, finely chopped
4 shallots, finely chopped
2 leeks (white part only), thinly sliced
1 fennel bulb, chopped
1/4 cup (1/2 stick) butter
2 tablespoons all-purpose flour
8 cups hot chicken stock
4 fresh tomatoes, peeled and chopped
2 (28-ounce) cans whole tomatoes

2 teaspoons fennel seeds
2 teaspoons anise seeds
1/4 cup sugar
Salt and black pepper to taste
1/4 teaspoon cayenne pepper
2 cups half-and-half

SAMBUCA CREAM

1 cup heavy whipping cream
1 teaspoon grated lemon zest
1/2 teaspoon lemon juice
1/4 cup sambuca or anisette, or to taste
2 tablespoons sugar

For the soup, heat the cottonseed oil in a large heavy saucepan. Stir in the bell peppers, onions, shallots, leeks and fennel. Cook, covered, until the vegetables are tender but not brown. Add the butter. Stir in the flour and cook for 1 minute; do not brown. Add the stock gradually, stirring constantly. Bring to a boil. Stir in the fresh tomatoes, canned tomatoes, fennel seeds and anise seeds. Simmer for 20 to 30 minutes. Remove from the heat.

Stir in the sugar, salt, black pepper and cayenne pepper. Purée the mixture in a food processor or blender. Strain the mixture through a sieve into the saucepan. Stir in the half-and-half. Cook until heated through.

For the cream, whip the cream in a bowl until stiff peaks form. Stir in the lemon zest, lemon juice, sambuca and sugar. Ladle the soup into serving bowls and serve with a dollop of the Sambuca Cream. *Serves 12.*

SPINACH BISQUE

2 (10-ounce) packages frozen chopped spinach
4 cups chicken broth
3 tablespoons chopped onion
1/2 cup (1 stick) butter

1/4 cup cornstarch
1 cup (4 ounces) shredded Cheddar cheese
2 cups half-and-half
1/4 cup (1 ounce) grated Parmesan cheese

Cook the spinach in the broth in a large saucepan for 10 to 15 minutes. Sauté the onion in the butter in a skillet until tender. Remove from the heat and let cool.

Stir in the cornstarch. Add to the spinach mixture. Stir in the Cheddar cheese, half-and-half and Parmesan cheese. Simmer until heated through. *Serves 6 to 8.*

ROQUEFORT AND SPINACH SOUP

1 onion, thinly sliced
2 tablespoons butter
1/3 cup brandy
6 cups chicken stock
9 ounces Roquefort cheese or
Maytag blue cheese, crumbled

1 (10-ounce) package fresh baby spinach, chopped
6 small plum tomatoes, peeled, seeded and chopped
3/4 teaspoon thyme
2 tablespoons butter
1 cup half-and-half or milk
Freshly ground white pepper

Sauté the onion in 2 tablespoons butter in a saucepan until golden brown. Remove from the heat and add the brandy. Ignite the brandy with a long match. Return the saucepan to the heat when the flames die out. Stir in the stock and cheese. Bring to a boil. Cook until the cheese is melted, stirring frequently. Remove from the heat; cool slightly. Purée the soup in a blender and return to the saucepan. Sauté the spinach, tomatoes and thyme in 2 tablespoons butter in a skillet for 2 to 3 minutes.

Add the spinach mixture to the soup. Stir in the half-and-half. Bring to a simmer over medium heat, stirring constantly. Season with white pepper. Ladle into soup bowls and garnish with Roquefort cheese or a baby spinach leaf. *Serves 8.*

Note: You may use one 10-ounce package frozen chopped spinach, thawed, drained and squeezed dry, instead of fresh spinach.

THAI COCONUT SQUASH SOUP

3 tablespoons peanut oil
3 shallots, thinly sliced
2 cups chicken broth
1 1/2 pounds kabocha or butternut squash, peeled and cut into 1/2-inch pieces (4 to 5 cups)

2 cups coconut milk
3 tablespoons fish sauce
1/4 cup chopped cilantro
2 teaspoons coarsely ground pepper
1 red serrano chile, thinly sliced

Heat the peanut oil in a saucepan over high heat until it starts to smoke. Add the shallots and sauté until golden brown. Reduce the heat and sauté for 20 minutes or until tender, adding 1/4 cup of the broth to prevent sticking, if necessary. Stir in the remaining broth, the squash and coconut milk.

Bring to a boil and reduce the heat. Simmer for 10 to 15 minutes or until the squash is tender. Remove from the heat and stir in the fish sauce. Add additional fish sauce or a pinch of salt, if desired. Ladle into soup bowls. Top each serving with equal portions of the cilantro, pepper and chile. *Serves 6.*

ZUCCHINI SOUP

2 onions, chopped
2 tablespoons butter
8 zucchini, chopped
2 russet or Yukon gold potatoes, peeled and chopped
$1/2$ teaspoon basil
$1/4$ teaspoon thyme
$1/4$ teaspoon rosemary
$1/4$ teaspoon white pepper
4 cups chicken broth
1 cup milk
$1/4$ cup instant potato flakes
1 tablespoon soy sauce

Sauté the onions in the butter in a large skillet until tender. Add the zucchini, potatoes, basil, thyme, rosemary and white pepper. Sauté for 5 minutes. Bring the broth to a boil in a saucepan. Stir in the zucchini mixture. Reduce the heat and simmer for 15 minutes. Remove from the heat and purée the soup in batches in a blender. Return the soup to the saucepan. Stir in the milk and return to a simmer.

Stir in the potato flakes and soy sauce. Adjust the seasonings. Garnish with $1/4$ cup chopped fresh dill weed. Serve hot or chilled. **Serves 8.**

Note: For more texture, purée only half the vegetables. You may also add carrots. Instead of using potato flakes, you may add another potato or use frozen hash brown potatoes. Adding cooked chicken makes this a hearty soup.

Most soups, with the exception of delicate fresh fruit soups, improve with time and can be made a day or two in advance. Leftovers freeze well.

CURRIED SQUASH SOUP

1 (12-ounce) package frozen cooked winter squash, thawed
2 cups nonfat chicken broth or vegetable broth
1 1/2 cups applesauce
1 to 2 teaspoons curry powder
1/2 teaspoon salt

Combine the squash, broth, applesauce, curry powder and salt in a saucepan. Cook until heated through, stirring occasionally. *Serves 4 to 6.*

Note: You may prepare this soup in the microwave, if desired.

TOMATO BASIL SOUP

A favorite from The Village Club's kitchen

1 1/2 onions, coarsely chopped
3 ribs celery, coarsely chopped
3 garlic cloves, coarsely chopped
1/2 bunch basil, coarsely chopped
2 tablespoons olive oil
3/4 cup white wine
3 cups rich chicken stock

6 cups tomato sauce
Salt to taste
1 teaspoon white pepper
6 tablespoons butter
6 tablespoons all-purpose flour
1 1/2 cups heavy cream
Chopped fresh basil

Sauté the onions, celery, garlic and basil in the olive oil in a large saucepan over medium heat until the vegetables are tender. Stir in the wine. Cook until the wine is reduced by half. Stir in the stock and bring to a boil. Stir in the tomato sauce and return to a boil. Reduce the heat and stir in the salt and white pepper. Simmer over low heat for 1 hour.

Melt the butter in a small skillet over medium-low heat. Stir in the flour. Cook until golden brown, stirring constantly. Whisk enough of the flour mixture into the soup to reach the desired thickness. Simmer for 30 minutes. Strain the soup into a saucepan and discard the vegetables. Bring to a simmer. Stir in the cream and basil and cook gently until heated through. *Serves 8.*

CONSOMME

A favorite recipe of a past president

---

¹/₃ cup finely diced (¹/₁₆ inch) carrot
¹/₃ cup finely diced (¹/₁₆ inch) onion
¹/₃ cup finely diced (¹/₁₆ inch) celery
¹/₃ cup finely diced (¹/₁₆ inch) leek (white part only)
¹/₃ cup finely diced (¹/₁₆ inch) white turnip
2 tablespoons butter
Salt and pepper to taste
8 cups canned consommé
3 to 4 tablespoons dry port, madeira or sherry, or to taste
3 to 4 tablespoons finely chopped fresh chervil,
parsley, chives or combination

Cook the carrot, onion, celery, leek and turnip in the butter in a covered saucepan over low heat until tender but not brown. Season with salt and pepper. Stir in 1 cup of the consommé and simmer for several minutes.

Stir in the remaining 7 cups consommé and return to a simmer. Adjust the seasonings. Remove from the heat and stir in the port. Ladle into a soup tureen or soup bowls and top with the herbs. *Serves 6.*

Note: For added flavor you can simmer the canned consommé beforehand with a little wine or dry white vermouth, some chopped onions, carrots, celery, and herbs to taste. Strain and reserve the liquid.

*T*he addition of wine frequently enhances the flavor of soup.
A not too dry sherry or madeira blends well with subtle veal or chicken,
while a little dry red table wine will complement the flavor of beef.

VEGETABLE BISQUE

A favorite from The Village Club's kitchen

1³/4 bunches asparagus, coarsely chopped
1 (8-ounce) package frozen peas, or about 1¹/2 cups fresh peas
¹/2 onion, coarsely chopped
1¹/2 garlic cloves, coarsely chopped
1 bunch fresh spinach, chopped, or
1 (16-ounce) package frozen chopped spinach
16 ounces corn kernels, or coarsely chopped zucchini or squash
Olive oil
1 cup white wine
8 cups chicken stock
1 cup heavy cream
¹/2 cup (1 stick) butter
Salt and pepper to taste
Grated Parmesan cheese

Sauté the asparagus, peas, onion, garlic, spinach and corn in olive oil in a large saucepan over medium-high heat until the vegetables are tender and slightly caramelized. Stir in the wine. Cook until the wine is reduced by half. Stir in the stock and bring to a boil.

Reduce the heat and simmer for 45 minutes. Remove from the heat and purée the soup with an immersion blender. Stir in the cream, butter, salt and pepper. Simmer for 30 minutes. Ladle into soup bowls and top with grated Parmesan cheese. *Serves 12.*

*A*ny soup that has a particular herb seasoning should receive a generous dash of that herb just before you are ready to purée. This gives the soup a fresher flavor.

DYNAMITE VEGETABLE CHOWDER

1¹/2 pounds zucchini
1 onion, chopped
2 tablespoons chopped fresh parsley
1 teaspoon basil
5¹/2 tablespoons butter
¹/3 cup all-purpose flour
1¹/2 teaspoons salt
¹/4 teaspoon pepper

1 tablespoon chicken bouillon granules
1 teaspoon lemon juice
3 cups water
1 (10-ounce) package frozen corn kernels
1³/4 cups evaporated milk
6 tomatoes, peeled, seeded and chopped
1 cup (4 ounces) shredded fontina cheese
¹/4 cup (1 ounce) grated Romano cheese

Cut the zucchini into halves lengthwise and then into 1-inch pieces. Sauté the zucchini, onion, parsley and basil in the butter in a large saucepan for 8 minutes or until the vegetables are tender. Stir in the flour, salt and pepper. Cook over low heat until bubbly, stirring constantly. Remove from the heat and stir in the bouillon granules, lemon juice and water. Return to the heat.

Bring to a boil, stirring constantly. Stir in the corn and reduce the heat. Simmer, covered, for 8 minutes. Stir in the evaporated milk and tomatoes. Return to a boil. Add the fontina cheese and Romano cheese and cook until the cheese is melted, stirring constantly. Serve immediately. *Serves 4 to 6.*

QUICK SUMMER MINESTRONE

10 cups chicken stock
8 mushrooms, sliced
4 carrots, sliced
1 (8-ounce) can garbanzo beans, drained
1 (8-ounce) can stewed tomatoes
1 (6-ounce) jar marinated artichoke hearts
2 small zucchini, sliced
1 onion, chopped

1 large celery heart with leaves, chopped
1 large tomato, peeled, seeded and chopped
¹/4 cup chopped fresh parsley
1 garlic clove, chopped
1 small bunch spinach, stems removed
1 cup broken vermicelli
Salt and freshly ground pepper to taste
Freshly grated Parmesan cheese

Stir the stock, mushrooms, carrots, garbanzo beans, stewed tomatoes, artichoke hearts, zucchini, onion, celery, tomato, parsley and garlic in a large saucepan. Cook, covered, over low heat for 30 minutes or until the vegetables are tender-crisp.

Stir in the spinach and vermicelli. Cook for 10 minutes. Season with salt and pepper.

Ladle the soup into soup bowls and top with Parmesan cheese. Serve immediately. *Serves 10.*

TUSCAN VEGETABLE SOUP

$1/4$ cup olive oil
1 cup chopped savoy cabbage
1 cup chopped red onion
1 carrot, chopped
1 rib celery, chopped
1 cup fresh green beans, chopped
1 package fresh spinach
2 teaspoons minced garlic
1 cup fresh basil leaves

1 cup chopped tomatoes
2 tablespoons tomato paste
$3/4$ cup uncooked coarsely chopped potatoes
4 cups chicken broth
Salt and pepper to taste
$1/2$ cup cannellini beans
$1/2$ cup cooked, chopped peeled potatoes
$1/4$ cup (1 ounce) grated Parmesan cheese

Heat the olive oil in a large saucepan. Stir in the cabbage, onion, carrot, celery, green beans, spinach, garlic and basil. Cook, covered, over medium heat until the vegetables are tender. Stir in the tomatoes, tomato paste, uncooked potatoes and broth. Bring to a boil and reduce the heat. Simmer for 30 minutes. Season with salt and pepper.

Purée the cannellini beans and cooked potatoes in a blender. Remove to a bowl and stir in the cheese. Stir the bean mixture into the soup. Add additional broth if the soup is too thick. Adjust the seasonings. *Serves 8 to 10.*

Note: This soup is best if made the day before serving. Chill, covered, in the refrigerator. Reheat before serving.

CHILLED HERBED CUCUMBER SOUP

3 tablespoons slivered blanched almonds
1¹/2 cups nonfat plain yogurt
1¹/2 cups buttermilk
¹/4 cup sour cream
1 English cucumber, shredded

¹/4 cup finely chopped fresh parsley
2 garlic cloves, minced
3 tablespoons finely chopped fresh mint
3 tablespoons finely chopped fresh dill weed
Salt and white pepper to taste

Sauté the almonds in a small skillet for 2 to 3 minutes or until golden brown. Remove to a plate. Combine the yogurt, buttermilk and sour cream in a bowl and mix well. Stir in the cucumber, parsley, garlic, mint, dill weed, salt and white pepper. Chill, covered, for 2 to 8 hours.

Adjust the seasonings. Ladle into chilled soup bowls and top with equal portions of the almonds. *Serves 6.*

Note: Peel and seed the cucumber if you are using a regular cucumber instead of an English cucumber.

CHILLED HUNGARIAN BERRY SOUP

1 (10- to 12-ounce) package frozen blueberries,
strawberries or raspberries
¹/4 cup sweet madeira, ruby port or cream sherry
2 (6-ounce) cartons fruit yogurt
1 (6-ounce) carton plain yogurt
2 tablespoons sugar, or to taste

Purée the blueberries, madeira, fruit yogurt and plain yogurt in a food processor, stopping once or twice to scrape down the sides.

Add the sugar and process for 15 seconds. Pour into stemmed goblets. Garnish each serving with an orange slice, mint sprig and a few fresh berries. *Serves 4 to 6.*

Avocado and Citrus Salad
with Pomegranate Seeds 49
Fig and Prosciutto Salad 49
Raspberry Orange Lettuce Salad 50
Dried Cherry and Toasted Pecan
Salad with Maple Dressing 51
Roquefort Pear Salad 52
Martha's Vineyard Salad 52
California Salad with Lemon Mustard
Dressing 53
Strawberry Salad with Poppy Seeds 54
Spinach and Apple Salad 54
Spinach Beet Salad with Roasted
Shallot Dressing 55
Broccoli Slaw 56

Layered Broccoli Salad 56
Brussels Sprouts and
Cherry Tomato Salad 57
Farm Fresh Corn Salad 57
Garden Corn and Black Bean Salad 58
Cold Sweet Potato Salad 58
Chicken Blueberry Salad 59
Condiment Chicken Salad 59
My Favorite Chicken Salad 60
Mexican Caesar Salad 60
Dilled Shrimp and Feta Cheese Salad 61
Shrimp Salad with Romaine 61
Quinoa and Black Bean Salad 62
Tabouli Salad 63
Cranberry Tabouli .63

SALADS
Salads

The setting on the facing page was designed and the accessories selected by Leslie Benser and
Liz Fallert of La Belle Provence, Birmingham, Michigan, and photographed by Yakov Faytlin in
The Village Club Winningham room.

3

SALADS

Salads

THE LIVING ROOM OF THE VILLAGE CLUB CIRCA 1961

Looking into the living room and sunroom from the front hall of The Winningham House shows one of six murals depicting scenes from the story of Robin Hood and his band of merry men. These murals and Charles Winningham's knowledge and fondness of Robin Hood lore gave the house the nickname of Robin Hood's Barn. When renovating, The Village Club donated the Robin Hood murals to a children's hospital. However, the original barn hayloft timbers still remain in the living room ceiling of the Club.

AVOCADO AND CITRUS SALAD WITH POMEGRANATE SEEDS

2 tablespoons honey
2 tablespoons fresh lime juice
2 cups loosely packed torn romaine
2 cups loosely packed torn radicchio
2 cups grapefruit sections (about 2 large grapefruit), or
4 oranges, sectioned
1/2 small red onion, sliced and separated into rings
1 avocado, sliced
1 cup pomegranate seeds

Combine the honey and lime juice in a small bowl and whisk to mix well. Chill, covered, in the refrigerator. Arrange 1/2 cup romaine and 1/2 cup radicchio on each of four salad plates.

Top each salad with equal portions of the grapefruit, onion and avocado. Sprinkle each with equal portions of the pomegranate seeds. Drizzle 1 tablespoon of the honey mixture over each salad and toss gently to coat. *Serves 4.*

FIG AND PROSCIUTTO SALAD

1/2 cup olive oil
1/4 cup white wine vinegar
1/2 garlic clove, finely chopped
1/8 teaspoon kosher salt

4 fresh figs, halved lengthwise
8 (heaping) teaspoons goat cheese
4 slices prosciutto, halved lengthwise
4 cups mixed baby greens

Combine the olive oil, vinegar, garlic and salt in a bowl and whisk to mix well.

Scoop 1 teaspoon of fruit from each fig half using a melon baller. Spoon 1 heaping teaspoon of goat cheese into each fig cavity. Wrap 1 piece of prosciutto around each fig half.

Arrange the figs on a baking sheet. Broil 2 inches from the heat source for 90 seconds per side or until the prosciutto begins to sizzle. Combine the greens and vinaigrette in a bowl and toss well. Divide evenly among four salad plates. Place two fig halves on each salad and serve immediately. *Serves 4.*

RASPBERRY ORANGE LETTUCE SALAD

RASPBERRY VINAIGRETTE

1/2 cup vegetable oil
1/4 cup raspberry vinegar
1/4 cup sugar
2 tablespoons finely chopped fresh parsley
1 teaspoon salt
1/2 teaspoon pepper
2 dashes of Tabasco sauce

SALAD

6 tablespoons sugar
1 cup slivered almonds
Red or green leaf lettuce, fresh spinach or romaine, torn into bite-size pieces
Sliced green onions
1 rib celery, sliced
1 (11-ounce) can mandarin oranges, drained, or fresh orange sections
Fresh raspberries

For the vinaigrette, process the oil, vinegar, sugar, parsley, salt, pepper and Tabasco sauce in a food processor or blender.

For the salad, heat the sugar in a skillet over medium heat. Add the almonds.

Cook until the sugar is melted and the almonds are coated, stirring constantly. Remove to waxed paper to cool. Combine the lettuce, green onions, celery, oranges, raspberries and almonds in a bowl and toss to mix. Add the vinaigrette and toss to coat. *Serves 6 to 8.*

To store green onions, cut the roots and trim the green tops to fit in a jar. Rinse and dry completely. Cover and store in the jar in the refrigerator. The onions will keep for weeks and will not get soft.

DRIED CHERRY AND TOASTED PECAN SALAD WITH MAPLE DRESSING

MAPLE DRESSING
$1/4$ cup mayonnaise
$1/4$ cup pure maple syrup
3 tablespoons Champagne vinegar or
white wine vinegar
2 teaspoons sugar
$1/2$ cup vegetable oil
Salt and pepper to taste

SALAD
1 bunch Bibb lettuce, torn into bite-size pieces
1 bunch red leaf lettuce, torn into bite-size pieces
$1/4$ cup toasted chopped pecans
$1/2$ cup dried tart cherries
$1/4$ cup toasted chopped pecans
1 red onion, thinly sliced

For the dressing, whisk the mayonnaise, maple syrup, vinegar and sugar in a bowl. Add the oil gradually, whisking constantly until the mixture is slightly thickened. Season with salt and pepper.

For the salad, combine the Bibb lettuce, red leaf lettuce, $1/4$ cup pecans and the dried cherries in a bowl and toss to mix well. Add the desired amount of the dressing and toss to coat. Divide the salad evenly among six salad plates. Sprinkle with $1/4$ cup pecans and top with the sliced onion. *Serves 6.*

ROQUEFORT PEAR SALAD

1/3 cup olive oil
3 tablespoons red wine vinegar
1 1/2 teaspoons sugar
1 1/2 teaspoons mustard
1 garlic clove, finely chopped
1/2 teaspoon salt
Freshly ground pepper to taste

1/4 cup sugar
1/2 cup pecans
1 head leaf lettuce, torn into bite-size pieces
3 pears, peeled, cored and chopped
5 ounces Roquefort cheese, crumbled
1 avocado, chopped
1/2 cup thinly sliced green onions

Whisk the olive oil, vinegar, 1 1/2 teaspoons sugar, the mustard, garlic, salt and pepper in a bowl.

Combine 1/4 cup sugar and the pecans in a skillet. Cook over medium heat until the sugar is melted and the pecans are coated, stirring constantly.

Remove the coated pecans to waxed paper to cool. Break apart the pecans when cool.

Layer the lettuce, pears, cheese, avocado and green onions in a bowl. Pour the dressing evenly over the salad and sprinkle with the pecans. *Serves 6.*

MARTHA'S VINEYARD SALAD

SALAD

2 heads Boston lettuce, torn into bite-size pieces
1 head radicchio, torn into bite-size pieces
1 red onion, sliced
8 ounces blue cheese, coarsely crumbled
1/2 cup pine nuts (toasted, if desired)

MARTHA'S VINEYARD DRESSING

1 teaspoon salt
1 teaspoon tarragon
1 teaspoon Dijon mustard
1/2 cup raspberry vinegar
1/2 cup olive oil
1/2 cup canola oil
1/2 cup pure maple syrup

For the salad, place the Boston lettuce and radicchio in a lettuce crisper and chill overnight. Combine the Boston lettuce, radicchio, onion, cheese and pine nuts in a bowl and toss to mix well.

For the dressing, mix the salt, tarragon and Dijon mustard in a bowl to make a paste. Whisk in the vinegar, olive oil, canola oil and maple syrup. Whisk for 10 to 15 seconds. Add to the salad and toss to coat. *Serves 8.*

CALIFORNIA SALAD WITH LEMON MUSTARD DRESSING

LEMON MUSTARD DRESSING
1 cup olive oil
$^1/_2$ cup lemon juice
1$^1/_2$ teaspoons Dijon mustard
1$^1/_2$ teaspoons honey
1 teaspoon Worcestershire sauce
$^1/_2$ teaspoon salt
Dash of white pepper

SALAD
1 large head romaine, torn into bite-size pieces
5 to 6 ounces seedless black grapes
2 oranges, peeled, sectioned and seeded
1 small red onion, sliced
1 avocado, sliced
Salt and pepper to taste

For the dressing, combine the olive oil, lemon juice, Dijon mustard, honey, Worcestershire sauce, salt and pepper in a jar with a tight-fitting lid and shake well. Chill for 2 hours or up to 2 weeks.

For the salad, combine the romaine, grapes, oranges, onion and avocado in a bowl and toss to mix. Add the dressing and toss to coat. Season with salt and pepper. *Serves 6.*

*I*f you want more juice from a lemon or lime, roll it on your countertop before cutting and squeezing it. Alternatively, microwave it for 10 to 15 seconds before cutting and squeezing it.

STRAWBERRY SALAD WITH POPPY SEEDS

3 tablespoons sugar
3 tablespoons light mayonnaise
2 tablespoons milk
1 tablespoon poppy seeds

1 tablespoon white vinegar
10 ounces romaine, torn into bite-size pieces
1 cup sliced strawberries
2 tablespoons toasted slivered almonds

Combine the sugar, mayonnaise, milk, poppy seeds and vinegar in a small bowl and whisk until blended. Combine the romaine and strawberries in a salad bowl.

Pour the poppy seed mixture over the salad. Add the almonds and toss to mix well. *Serves 4.*

SPINACH AND APPLE SALAD

$1/4$ cup balsamic vinegar
$1/4$ cup pure maple syrup
$1/4$ cup olive oil
$1/4$ teaspoon salt
$1/4$ teaspoon pepper

2 (6-ounce) packages fresh spinach
2 tart green apples, cored and thinly sliced
8 ounces extra-sharp white Cheddar cheese, cut into $1/2$-inch cubes
$1/2$ cup chopped toasted walnuts

Whisk the vinegar, maple syrup, olive oil, salt and pepper in a bowl, or combine in a jar with a tight-fitting lid and shake well. Combine the spinach, apples, cheese and walnuts in a bowl. Add enough dressing to coat and toss gently to mix. *Serves 8.*

Note: The dressing can be made several days in advance. Whisk or shake before using.

SPINACH BEET SALAD WITH ROASTED SHALLOT DRESSING

2 shallots
1 teaspoon olive oil
1/4 cup olive oil
1 tablespoon balsamic vinegar
1/4 teaspoon salt
1/4 teaspoon pepper
2 small beets
2 teaspoons olive oil
3 cups fresh baby spinach leaves
1/2 small fennel bulb, trimmed and thinly sliced
(about 1 cup)
1/4 cup coarsely chopped toasted walnuts
1 ounce goat cheese

Peel the shallots and place in a small foil-lined baking pan. Drizzle with 1 teaspoon olive oil. Seal the foil around the shallots. Bake at 450 degrees for 20 minutes or until tender and golden brown. Remove the shallots to a cutting board. Chop when cool. Whisk the shallots, 1/4 cup olive oil, vinegar, salt and pepper in a bowl.

Rinse the beets and place in a small foil-lined baking pan. Drizzle with 2 teaspoons olive oil. Seal the foil around the beets.

Bake at 450 degrees for 25 to 30 minutes or until tender. Remove the beets to a cutting board. Peel and slice when cool. Combine the beets and half the dressing in a bowl and toss to coat. Combine the spinach and remaining dressing in a bowl and toss to coat. Divide the spinach evenly among four to six salad plates. Top with equal portions of the beets and fennel. Sprinkle each salad with the walnuts and top with a dollop of the cheese. *Serves 4 to 6.*

Salads

BROCCOLI SLAW

2 (3-ounce) packages chicken-flavored ramen noodles
$^1/_2$ cup sugar
$^3/_4$ cup vegetable oil
2 tablespoons red wine vinegar
1 package broccoli slaw
1 bunch green onions, chopped
$^1/_2$ cup sunflower seeds
$^3/_4$ cup slivered almonds

Remove the seasoning packets from the ramen noodles. Crumble the noodles and set aside. Whisk the contents of the seasoning packets with the sugar, oil and vinegar in a bowl.

Combine the broccoli slaw and green onions in a bowl. Add the sunflower seeds, almonds and ramen noodles. Add the dressing and toss to coat. Chill until serving time. *Serves 4 to 6.*

LAYERED BROCCOLI SALAD

6 cups chopped broccoli florets
1 small red onion, very thinly sliced
$^2/_3$ cup sweetened dried cranberries
$^1/_2$ cup fat-free plain yogurt
3 tablespoons honey
2 tablespoons mayonnaise
2 tablespoons cider vinegar
$1^1/_2$ cups (6 ounces) shredded reduced-fat Cheddar cheese
$^1/_4$ cup unsalted dry roasted sunflower seeds
2 tablespoons reduced-fat bacon bits

Layer the broccoli, onion and dried cranberries in a glass serving dish. Whisk the yogurt, honey, mayonnaise and vinegar in a small bowl. Pour evenly over the salad.

Sprinkle the cheese evenly over the top. Chill, covered, until serving time. Sprinkle the sunflower seeds and bacon bits evenly over the top just before serving. *Serves 8.*

BRUSSELS SPROUTS AND CHERRY TOMATO SALAD

1 cup vegetable oil
1/4 cup red wine vinegar
1 teaspoon mustard
1 teaspoon Worcestershire sauce
1 teaspoon sugar
1 teaspoon salt
1/2 teaspoon basil

1/4 teaspoon thyme
1/4 teaspoon pepper
1 1/4 pounds brussels sprouts,
  trimmed and halved lengthwise
2 cups cherry tomatoes, halved lengthwise
1/2 cup thinly sliced green onions

Combine the oil, vinegar, mustard, Worcestershire sauce, sugar, salt, basil, thyme and pepper in a jar with a tight-fitting lid and shake well.

Add the brussels sprouts to a 3- to 4-quart saucepan of lightly salted water. Bring to a boil and cook for 7 minutes or just until tender-crisp.

Drain the brussels sprouts in a colander and remove to a bowl. Pour the dressing over the warm brussels sprouts and toss to coat. Chill, covered, for 4 hours to overnight. Add the tomatoes and green onions to the brussels sprouts and mix gently. Remove to a serving dish. *Serves 6 to 8.*

FARM FRESH CORN SALAD

5 ears of fresh corn, husked, cooked, cooled and
cut off the cob
1 small red onion, chopped
3 tablespoons white vinegar
3 tablespoons olive oil

Mix the corn and onion in a bowl. Whisk the vinegar and olive oil in a bowl. Add to the corn mixture and toss to coat. Adjust the seasonings. Chill, covered, for 1 hour or longer. Serve with grilled meat. *Serves 4.*

Note: Chopped radicchio, chopped bell peppers, sliced seedless cucumbers, julienned zucchini or grape tomatoes make nice additions to this salad.

GARDEN CORN AND BLACK BEAN SALAD

3/4 cup reduced-calorie Italian
salad dressing
2 tablespoons finely chopped fresh
cilantro or parsley
2 tablespoons lime juice
1/2 teaspoon hot red pepper sauce
1 garlic clove, minced
3/4 teaspoon cumin
Salt to taste
1 tablespoon olive oil

4 ears of fresh corn, kernels removed, or
2 cups frozen corn kernels, thawed
1 jalapeño chile, seeded and finely chopped
1 (15-ounce) can black beans, drained and rinsed
1 (15-ounce) can hearts of palm, drained and
cut into bite-size pieces
1 large red bell pepper, cut into 1-inch pieces
1 cup cherry tomatoes, cut into halves
4 green onions, cut into 1/2-inch pieces
1/2 cup chopped red onion

Combine the salad dressing, cilantro, lime juice, hot sauce, garlic, cumin and salt in a jar with a tight-fitting lid and shake well.

Heat the olive oil in a skillet over medium-high heat. Add the corn and jalapeño and sauté for 3 to 4 minutes or until light brown. Remove to a large bowl and cool slightly.

Stir in the beans, hearts of palm, bell pepper, tomatoes, green onions and red onion. Add the dressing and toss to coat. Chill, covered, for 6 hours to overnight. Toss lightly and remove to a serving dish. *Serves 8.*

Note: This salad keeps well and is delicious for summer barbecues.

COLD SWEET POTATO SALAD

4 (small to medium) sweet potatoes
1/2 cup chopped red bell pepper
1/2 cup chopped celery
1/2 cup chopped fresh pineapple

3/4 cup mayonnaise
1/4 cup Dijon mustard
1/3 cup chopped pecans
Finely chopped fresh chives

Cook the sweet potatoes just until slightly tender; do not overcook. Let cool. Peel and chop the sweet potatoes. Combine the sweet potatoes, bell pepper, celery and pineapple in a bowl and toss gently.

Combine the mayonnaise and Dijon mustard in a bowl and mix well. Add enough of the mayonnaise mixture to the potatoes to coat and toss gently. Fold in the pecans and sprinkle with chives. *Serves 4 to 6.*

CHICKEN BLUEBERRY SALAD

2 cups chopped cooked chicken
2 cups chopped celery
1 (11-ounce) can mandarin oranges, drained
1/2 cup seedless green grapes
1/4 cup slivered sweet pickles
3/4 cup mayonnaise

Grated zest of 1 lime
Juice of 1 lime
1/2 teaspoon salt
Romaine leaves
1/2 cup toasted slivered almonds
1 cup fresh blueberries

Combine the chicken, celery, oranges, grapes and pickles in a bowl and toss to mix. Combine the mayonnaise, lime zest, lime juice and salt in a bowl and mix well.

Add the mayonnaise mixture to the chicken mixture and stir gently. Line a serving dish with romaine leaves. Add the chicken mixture. Top with the almonds and blueberries. *Serves 4.*

CONDIMENT CHICKEN SALAD

1 cup raisins
White wine
1 cup mango chutney
1 1/2 cups mayonnaise
1 cup salted peanuts
1 cup flaked coconut
2 pounds cooked chicken, coarsely chopped

2 cups diagonally sliced bananas
Salt and pepper to taste
Salad greens
Avocado slices
Banana slices
Lemon juice

Plump the raisins in wine in a small bowl for a few hours. Drain and place the raisins in a large bowl. Slice the fruit in the chutney into slivers. Add to the raisins. Add the mayonnaise, peanuts and coconut and mix well. Add the chicken and toss to mix. Add 2 cups banana slices, salt and pepper and toss gently. Spoon the chicken salad into a large serving dish or onto a platter lined with salad greens.

Dip avocado and banana slices in lemon juice and arrange around the chicken salad. *Serves 12.*

Note: You may use slices of melon, pineapple, mango or other fruit around the salad instead of banana and avocado, or use any combination desired.

MY FAVORITE CHICKEN SALAD

A Village Club favorite from Food With A Flair *and a favorite recipe from a past president*

6 large chicken breasts
Sliced carrot, chopped onion and chopped
celery with leaves
1 (6-ounce) can blanched almonds
Butter
1 cup each seedless green grapes and chopped celery

4 hard-cooked eggs, coarsely chopped
4 teaspoons capers
12 pitted ripe olives, slivered
2 cups mayonnaise
2 tablespoons heavy cream
Salt, pepper and paprika to taste

Simmer the chicken, carrot, onion and celery in a saucepan of water until the chicken is cooked through. Chill, covered, overnight. Drain, discarding the broth and vegetables. Cut the chicken into bite-size pieces. Brown the almonds in butter in a skillet; cool.

Combine the chicken, almonds, grapes, 1 cup chopped celery, the eggs, capers and olives in a bowl and mix well. Combine the mayonnaise, cream, salt, pepper and paprika in a bowl and mix well. Add to the chicken salad and mix gently. Serve on lettuce-lined plates. *Serves 8.*

MEXICAN CAESAR SALAD

MEXICAN CAESAR DRESSING

1/2 cup mayonnaise
1/4 cup chopped green onions
1 tablespoon Dijon mustard
1/4 cup crumbled queso fresco (Mexican cheese)
1/4 cup each chopped cilantro and fresh lime juice
3 anchovy fillets, mashed or finely chopped
1/2 teaspoon finely chopped garlic
1 teaspoon pepper
1/2 teaspoon salt

SALAD

1 large head romaine, torn into 1-inch pieces
3 cups cooked chile-rubbed chicken strips
Tortilla strips (optional)
1 cup julienned roasted red bell pepper
4 ounces queso fresco (Mexican cheese),
  crumbled
4 cilantro sprigs

For the dressing, whisk the mayonnaise, green onions, Dijon mustard, cheese, cilantro, lime juice, anchovies, garlic, pepper and salt in a bowl.

For the salad, combine the romaine, chicken and tortilla strips in a bowl and toss to mix.

Add the dressing; toss to coat. Top with the roasted bell pepper, cheese and cilantro and serve immediately. *Serves 6.*

Note: To make tortilla strips, fry 1/4-inch strips of flour tortillas in hot oil in an iron skillet until golden brown. Remove to paper towels to drain.

DILLED SHRIMP AND FETA CHEESE SALAD

1 pound cooked shrimp, peeled and chilled
3 green onions with tops, thinly sliced
1/2 cucumber, peeled, seeded and chopped
1 (4-ounce) jar diced pimento or
diced red bell pepper
2 tablespoons finely chopped fresh
dill weed or parsley

1/4 cup (about 1 ounce) crumbled feta cheese
2 tablespoons lemon juice
2 tablespoons olive oil
1 tablespoon white wine vinegar
1 teaspoon Dijon mustard or spicy brown mustard
1 garlic clove, minced
1/4 teaspoon pepper

Combine the shrimp, green onions, cucumber, pimento, dill weed and cheese in a bowl. Combine the lemon juice, olive oil, vinegar, Dijon mustard, garlic and pepper in a small bowl.

Whisk the lemon juice mixture until smooth. Pour evenly over the shrimp mixture and toss gently to coat. *Serves 4.*

SHRIMP SALAD WITH ROMAINE

1 (15-ounce) can hearts of palm, drained and
cut into 1/2-inch pieces
5 to 6 ounces cooked shrimp, peeled and
cut into bite-size pieces
2 tablespoons white wine vinegar
1/4 cup olive oil
3 tablespoons finely chopped green onion tops
1 bunch romaine, thinly sliced

Combine the hearts of palm, shrimp, vinegar, olive oil and green onion tops in a bowl and toss to mix. Chill, covered, for 5 hours to overnight.

Divide the romaine evenly among four to six salad plates. Top with equal portions of the shrimp salad. *Serves 4 to 6.*

QUINOA AND BLACK BEAN SALAD

1¹/2 cups quinoa
1¹/2 cups canned black beans, drained and rinsed
4¹/2 teaspoons red wine vinegar
Pinch of salt
Dash of black pepper
1¹/2 cups cooked fresh or frozen corn kernels
1 red bell pepper, seeded and chopped

6 scallions, chopped
1 teaspoon minced garlic
¹/4 teaspoon cayenne pepper
¹/4 cup cilantro, finely chopped
¹/3 cup fresh lime juice
1¹/2 teaspoons cumin
¹/2 teaspoon salt
¹/3 cup olive oil

Cook the quinoa according to the package directions. Fluff with a fork and remove to a bowl to cool.

Combine the beans, vinegar, pinch of salt and dash of black pepper in a large bowl and toss to mix. Add the corn, bell pepper, scallions, garlic, cayenne pepper, cilantro and quinoa and toss to mix.

Whisk the lime juice, cumin and ¹/2 teaspoon salt in a small bowl. Add the olive oil in a steady stream, whisking constantly. Adjust the seasonings. Add to the quinoa mixture and toss to mix. Serve immediately or chill, covered, in the refrigerator. Bring to room temperature before serving. *Serves 14.*

Quinoa, the "mother grain" of the Incas, has a light, delicate, nutty taste and contains a more complete protein than other grains, plus a high level of vitamins and minerals. Quinoa can be found at specialty markets, some supermarkets, and health-food stores.

TABOULI SALAD

1/4 cup medium-grind cracked wheat
2 bunches (4 cups) fresh parsley, stems removed
1 bunch green onions, cut into 2-inch pieces
1/2 to 1 cup fresh mint, finely chopped
1 green bell pepper, finely chopped

1/2 cup olive oil
1/3 cup lemon juice
Garlic powder to taste
Salt and pepper to taste
4 tomatoes, seeded and finely chopped

Combine the wheat with enough cold water to cover in a bowl. Let stand for 15 to 20 minutes. Drain, squeeze dry and place in a large bowl. Process the well-drained parsley in a food processor until finely chopped. Add to the wheat. Process the green onions in a food processor until finely chopped. Add to the wheat mixture.

Add the mint and bell pepper to the wheat mixture. Combine the olive oil, lemon juice, garlic powder, salt and pepper in a bowl and whisk to mix well. Add to the wheat mixture and toss to mix. Spoon into a serving dish. Arrange the tomatoes around the inside rim of the dish. *Serves 6.*

CRANBERRY TABOULI

A favorite from The Village Club's kitchen

1 cup bulgur wheat
1/2 cup chopped dried cranberries
1 cup boiling water
1/2 cup chopped fresh parsley
1/4 cup finely chopped red onion
1/4 cup fresh lemon juice

2 tablespoons chopped fresh mint
4 1/2 teaspoons walnut oil
3/4 teaspoon salt
1/4 teaspoon freshly ground pepper
2 tablespoons toasted chopped walnuts (optional)

Combine the bulgur, dried cranberries and boiling water in a bowl. Let stand for 30 minutes or until the water is absorbed.

Fluff the bulgur mixture with a fork. Add the parsley, onion, lemon juice, mint, walnut oil, salt, pepper and walnuts and toss gently to mix. *Serves 6.*

Quick Quiche 67

Spinach Quiche .67

Asparagus Frittata 68

Cheese Soufflé 68

Chicken Soufflé .69

Chile Relleno Casserole 69

Savory Bread Pudding with
   Spring Herbs .70

Gougère 71

Lemon Bread 71

Pumpkin Bread .72

Wheat Germ Zucchini Bread 72

Banana Date Nut Muffins 73

Cherry Oatmeal Muffins 73

The Village Club Popovers 74

Buttermilk Date Orange Scones 74

Lemon Blueberry Biscuits 75

Two Ways to Make French Toast 76

Deluxe Pancake Mix 77

Favorite Pancake 77

Cake That Won't Last 78

Cinnamon Pecan Coffee Cake 78

Sour Cream Orange
   Coffee Cake 79

Blueberry Buckle 80

Hot Curried Fruit 80

Breakfast Cookies 81

Granola 81

BRUNCH
Brunch

The accessories on the facing page were provided by The Fuchsia Frog, Birmingham, Michigan, and the setting was photographed by Yakov Faytlin in The Village Club foyer.

4

BRUNCH

Brunch

THE FRONT HALL OF THE VILLAGE CLUB CIRCA 1961

The floor of the Winningham front hall contained Mercer tile, a fine tile made in Doylestown, Pennsylvania, in the genre of Pewabic tile which is still locally produced in Detroit, Michigan. Near the windows, overlooking the gardens, was a small hidden cupboard just large enough to hold a very young Miss Winningham, who would hide and then surprise guests as they entered the house. The lobby of The Village Club is still graced by the tile floor and the walls of wormy chestnut holding the original pewter sconces in a folded linen design and, yes, the hidden cupboard.

QUICK QUICHE

A Village Club favorite from Food With A Flair

3 eggs, lightly beaten
1 cup sour cream
3/4 teaspoon salt
1/2 teaspoon Worcestershire sauce

8 slices bacon, crisp-cooked and crumbled
1 cup (4 ounces) shredded Swiss cheese
1 (3-ounce) can French-fried onions
1 baked (9-inch) pie shell

Combine the eggs and sour cream in a bowl and mix well. Stir in the salt and Worcestershire sauce. Add the bacon, cheese and French-fried onions and mix well.

Pour the egg mixture into the pie shell. Bake at 300 degrees for 30 minutes. *Serves 6.*

SPINACH QUICHE

1 (9-ounce) package frozen spinach soufflé, thawed
2 eggs, lightly beaten
3 tablespoons milk
1/2 cup sliced mushrooms, cooked and drained
3 tablespoons chopped shallots

3/4 cup (about 4 ounces) crumbled cooked Italian sausage
3/4 cup (3 ounces) shredded Swiss cheese
1/4 teaspoon nutmeg
1 unbaked (9-inch) pie shell

Mix the spinach soufflé, eggs, milk, mushrooms, shallots, sausage, cheese and nutmeg in a bowl. Pour into the pie shell.

Bake the quiche at 400 degrees for 25 to 30 minutes or until a knife inserted into the center comes out clean. *Serves 6.*

You may test an egg for freshness by placing it in a deep bowl of water. If it lies on the bottom, it's fresh. If it stands on end, it's a little older, but edible. If it floats to the surface, dispose of it—it's spoiled.

ASPARAGUS FRITTATA

8 ounces asparagus
6 eggs
3 tablespoons chopped fresh parsley
2 tablespoons chopped fresh basil
Salt and pepper to taste

1/4 cup (1 ounce) grated Parmesan cheese
1/2 cup chopped red onion
1 garlic clove, minced
3 tablespoons olive oil
1/4 cup (1 ounce) grated Parmesan cheese

Cook the asparagus in water to cover in a saucepan over medium-high heat for 4 to 5 minutes or until tender; drain. Cut the asparagus into 1 1/2-inch pieces. Beat the eggs in a bowl just until blended. Add the asparagus, parsley, basil, salt, pepper and 1/4 cup cheese and mix well.

Sauté the onion and garlic in the olive oil in an ovenproof skillet or sauté pan until tender. Add the egg mixture and cook until set.

Sprinkle 1/4 cup cheese over the top of the frittata and broil until brown. *Serves 3.*

CHEESE SOUFFLE

A Village Club favorite from **Food With A Flair**

8 slices bread, thickly buttered and cut into cubes
8 ounces sharp Cheddar cheese, shredded
6 eggs, well beaten
1 teaspoon finely chopped onion
1 teaspoon brown sugar

1/2 teaspoon dry mustard
1/2 teaspoon salt
1/2 teaspoon cayenne pepper
1/4 teaspoon paprika
2 1/2 cups half-and-half

Alternate layers of the bread and cheese in a buttered baking dish, ending with cheese. Combine the eggs, onion, brown sugar, dry mustard, salt, cayenne pepper and paprika in a bowl and mix well. Add the half-and-half and mix well. Pour evenly over the prepared layers. Chill, covered, overnight. Let stand at room temperature for 30 minutes before baking. Place the baking dish in a larger baking pan.

Add enough hot water to the baking pan to come halfway up the sides of the baking dish. Bake at 350 degrees for 20 minutes. Reduce the oven temperature to 300 degrees and bake for 1 hour and 10 minutes. *Serves 10.*

Note: This may be frozen before baking. Thaw in the refrigerator before baking.

CHICKEN SOUFFLE

A favorite recipe from a past president

6 thin slices bread, cut into cubes
2 cups chopped cooked chicken
1/2 cup chopped onion
1/2 cup chopped celery
1/2 cup chopped green bell pepper
1/2 cup mayonnaise
Salt and pepper to taste

2 eggs, beaten
1 1/2 cups milk
4 slices bread, crusts trimmed and
   bread cubed
1 (10-ounce) can cream of mushroom soup
1/2 cup (2 ounces) shredded sharp
   Cheddar cheese

Spread 6 cubed bread slices over the bottom of a buttered baking dish. Combine the chicken, onion, celery, bell pepper, mayonnaise, salt and pepper in a bowl and mix well. Spoon over the bread cubes. Combine the eggs and milk in a bowl and mix well.

Pour the egg mixture evenly over the chicken mixture. Chill, covered, overnight.

Top the soufflé with 4 cubed bread slices. Spoon the soup over the bread and sprinkle with the cheese. Bake at 325 degrees for 1 hour. *Serves 4 to 6.*

CHILE RELLENO CASSEROLE

1 (7-ounce) can green chiles, drained
16 ounces shredded Cheddar cheese
8 ounces shredded Monterey Jack cheese
4 eggs

2 tablespoons all-purpose flour or cornstarch
1 (12-ounce) can evaporated milk
1/2 teaspoon salt
1/2 teaspoon pepper

Cut the chiles lengthwise into halves. Arrange half the chiles in a single layer in a greased baking dish. Sprinkle with half the Cheddar cheese and half the Monterey Jack cheese. Top with the remaining chiles. Sprinkle with the remaining Cheddar cheese and remaining Monterey Jack cheese. Combine the eggs, flour, milk, salt and pepper in a bowl and beat until smooth.

Pour the egg mixture evenly over the cheese layer. Bake at 350 degrees for 45 minutes or until light brown. *Serves 6.*

Note: This tasty brunch or luncheon dish can be served with a chunky medium salsa and cooked turkey sausage.

SAVORY BREAD PUDDING WITH SPRING HERBS

12 to 16 thick slices dry French or Italian bread
2¹/2 to 3 cups milk
1 pound asparagus, trimmed and
cut diagonally into ³/8×2-inch pieces
5 eggs
1 teaspoon salt
1 teaspoon freshly ground pepper

¹/2 cup chopped mixed herbs
(such as chives, rosemary, parsley, marjoram,
thyme and sage)
4 ounces Swiss cheese, shredded
4 ounces fontina cheese, shredded
¹/4 cup (1 ounce) freshly grated Romano cheese
1 tablespoon butter, cut into very small pieces

Place the bread in a single layer in a shallow dish. Pour 2¹/2 cups of the milk evenly over the bread. Let stand for 30 minutes or until the milk is absorbed. Press on the bread and remove the excess milk to a measuring cup. Add additional milk if needed to make ¹/2 cup. Set the milk and soaked bread aside. Place the asparagus in a steamer over boiling water in a saucepan. Steam for 2 to 3 minutes or until tender-crisp. Remove to a colander and rinse under cold water; drain. Remove and reserve six to eight pieces of asparagus. Combine the eggs, salt, pepper and the reserved ¹/2 cup milk in a bowl and beat until well mixed. Place one-third of the soaked bread in a buttered 3-quart soufflé dish.

Top with one-third of the asparagus, one-third of the herbs, one-third of the Swiss cheese, one-third of the fontina cheese and one-third of the Romano cheese. Pour one-third of the egg mixture evenly over the layers. Repeat the layers two times, using the remaining bread, asparagus, herbs, Swiss cheese, fontina cheese, Romano cheese and egg mixture. Sprinkle the reserved asparagus over the top. Dot with the butter. Bake at 350 degrees for 45 minutes or until the top is golden brown and a knife inserted near the center comes out clean. *Serves 6.*

Note: Served with slices of smoked ham or grilled salmon, this is a delicious luncheon dish.

*B*efore grating cheese, brush vegetable oil on the grater and it will clean up much easier.

GOUGERE

1 cup milk
1/4 cup (1/2 stick) butter
1/2 teaspoon salt
Dash of cayenne pepper

1 cup all-purpose flour
4 eggs
1 cup (4 ounces) shredded Swiss cheese

Combine the milk, butter, salt and cayenne pepper in a saucepan. Bring to a boil over medium heat. Add the flour all at once. Cook for 2 minutes or until the mixture pulls away from the side of the saucepan, stirring constantly with a vigorous motion. Remove from the heat and cool slightly. Beat in the eggs one at a time. Beat by hand until the mixture is smooth and shiny. Beat in half the cheese. Let cool to room temperature. Reserve one-fourth of the dough. Spoon seven equal portions of the remaining dough in a connected circle on a greased baking sheet.

Make seven equal-size balls from the reserved dough and place one ball on top of each mound. Sprinkle the mounds with the remaining cheese.

Bake at 375 degrees on the middle rack of the oven for 45 to 55 minutes or until crisp and golden brown. Do not open the oven door while baking. Serve hot with butter. *Serves 7.*

Note: The baked gougère can be stored in an airtight container. Crisp in a 300-degree oven just before serving.

LEMON BREAD

2 1/4 cups all-purpose flour
1/4 teaspoon salt
1/4 teaspoon baking soda
3/4 cup (1 1/2 sticks) butter, softened
1 1/2 cups sugar
3 eggs

3/4 cup buttermilk, plain yogurt or lemon yogurt
Grated zest of 1 lemon
3/4 cup chopped nuts (optional)
Juice of 1 lemon
1/4 cup sugar

Sift the flour, salt and baking soda together. Beat the butter and 1 1/2 cups sugar in a bowl until light and fluffy. Beat in the eggs. Stir in the dry ingredients alternately with the buttermilk. Stir in the lemon zest and nuts. Pour into a greased 5×9-inch loaf pan. Bake at 325 degrees for 1 hour and 20 minutes or until the bread tests done. Cool in the pan for 10 minutes. Remove to a wire rack to cool completely.

Pierce the entire top surface of the bread with a wooden pick. Combine the lemon juice and 1/4 cup sugar in a bowl. Stir until the sugar is dissolved. Pour over the top of the bread and let drip down the sides. *Serves 10.*

*Note: For **Orange Bread**, use orange zest and orange juice instead of lemon. This bread can also be made into muffins, and it freezes well.*

PUMPKIN BREAD

A Village Club favorite from Food With a Flair *and a favorite recipe from a past president*

4 eggs, beaten
3 cups sugar
1 cup vegetable oil
2/3 cup water
2 teaspoons vanilla extract
2 cups canned pumpkin
3 1/2 cups all-purpose flour

1 1/2 teaspoons salt
2 teaspoons baking soda
2 teaspoons ground cinnamon
1 teaspoon ground allspice
1 1/2 cups chopped nuts
1 cup chopped dates

Combine the eggs, sugar, oil, water, vanilla and pumpkin in a large bowl and mix well. Add the flour, salt, baking soda, cinnamon and allspice and mix well. Stir in the nuts and dates. Pour into three greased 5×9-inch loaf pans.

Bake at 350 degrees for 50 minutes or until the loaves test done. Remove to a wire rack to cool. *Serves 30.*

Note: This bread will remain fresh and moist for a week if wrapped well and kept in the refrigerator.

WHEAT GERM ZUCCHINI BREAD

2 1/2 cups all-purpose flour
1/2 cup wheat germ
1 tablespoon ground cinnamon
2 teaspoons baking soda
1/2 teaspoon baking powder
1 teaspoon salt
4 eggs

1 cup granulated sugar
1 cup packed brown sugar
1 cup vegetable oil
1 tablespoon vanilla extract
2 cups shredded zucchini
1 cup chopped nuts
Sesame seeds

Mix the flour, wheat germ, cinnamon, baking soda, baking powder and salt together. Beat the eggs in a bowl with an electric mixer. Add the granulated sugar, brown sugar, oil and vanilla and beat until thick and foamy. Stir in the zucchini and nuts. Fold in the dry ingredients.

Pour into two greased and floured 5×9-inch loaf pans. Sprinkle with sesame seeds.

Bake at 350 degrees for 1 hour or until the loaves test done. Remove to a wire rack to cool. This bread freezes well. *Serves 20.*

BANANA DATE NUT MUFFINS

1 cup all-purpose flour
1 cup whole wheat flour
$1/3$ cup sugar
2 teaspoons baking powder
$1/4$ teaspoon salt
$1/4$ teaspoon ground cinnamon

2 eggs, beaten
$1/4$ cup vegetable oil
$1/4$ cup fat-free plain yogurt
$3/4$ to 1 cup coarsely mashed banana
$3/4$ to 1 cup coarsely chopped dates
$1/2$ cup coarsely chopped walnuts

Mix the all-purpose flour, whole wheat flour, sugar, baking powder, salt and cinnamon in a bowl. Whisk the eggs, oil, yogurt and banana in a bowl. Stir in the dry ingredients; the batter will be thick.

Stir in the dates and walnuts. Fill greased muffin cups with batter.

Bake at 400 degrees for 15 to 18 minutes. Remove to a wire rack to cool. *Serves 12.*

CHERRY OATMEAL MUFFINS

1 cup quick-cooking oats
1 cup all-purpose flour
$1/2$ cup packed brown sugar
$1 1/2$ teaspoons baking powder
$1/2$ teaspoon ground cinnamon
$1/2$ teaspoon salt

1 cup dried cherries
$3/4$ cup buttermilk
1 egg, lightly beaten
$1/4$ cup vegetable oil
1 teaspoon almond extract

Combine the oats, flour, brown sugar, baking powder, cinnamon and salt in a bowl and mix well. Stir in the dried cherries. Combine the buttermilk, egg, oil and almond extract in a bowl and mix well.

Add the buttermilk mixture to the oat mixture and stir just until blended. Fill muffin cups two-thirds full with batter. Bake at 400 degrees for 15 to 20 minutes. *Serves 12.*

THE VILLAGE CLUB POPOVERS

A favorite from The Village Club's kitchen

5 eggs	1/4 teaspoon salt
4 cups milk	1/4 teaspoon sugar
5 1/2 cups all-purpose flour	3 teaspoons vegetable oil

Beat the eggs and milk in a bowl. Stir in the flour, salt and sugar. Chill, covered, for 24 hours. Place 1/4 teaspoon of the oil in each of twelve popover tins or cups. Fill the popover tins three-quarters full with batter. Bake at 325 degrees for 1 hour and 15 minutes. *Serves 12.*

Note: If baking a smaller batch of popovers, keep the batter chilled until ready to bake. Nonstick popover tins may be filled with batter and chilled overnight before baking.

BUTTERMILK DATE ORANGE SCONES

3 cups all-purpose flour	3/4 cup chopped dates
1/3 cup sugar	1 teaspoon grated orange zest
2 1/2 teaspoons baking powder	1 cup buttermilk
1/2 teaspoon baking soda	1/4 teaspoon ground cinnamon
3/4 teaspoon salt	2 tablespoons sugar
3/4 cup (1 1/2 sticks) chilled butter, cut into small pieces	1 tablespoon heavy cream or milk

Combine the flour, 1/3 cup sugar, the baking powder, baking soda and salt in a bowl and mix well. Cut in the butter with a pastry blender or fork until crumbly. Stir in the dates and orange zest. Make a well in the center of the dry ingredients and pour in the buttermilk. Stir with a fork just until moistened. Turn out onto a lightly floured work surface. Pat the dough into a 1/2-inch-thick circle. Cut with a 2 1/2-inch heart-shaped cutter or biscuit cutter. Place 1 1/2 inches apart on a lightly greased baking sheet.

Mix the cinnamon and 2 tablespoons sugar in a bowl. Brush the tops of the scones with cream and sprinkle with the cinnamon-sugar.

Bake at 400 to 425 degrees for 12 minutes or until light brown. Serve warm. *Serves 18.*

Note: These scones freeze well. You may use dried cranberries instead of the dates or use blueberries and lemon zest instead of the dates and orange zest.

LEMON BLUEBERRY BISCUITS

1 egg, lightly beaten
1 cup lemon yogurt
1 teaspoon grated lemon zest
2 cups all-purpose flour
$1/4$ cup granulated sugar
2 teaspoons baking powder
$1/2$ teaspoon baking soda
$1/4$ teaspoon salt

$1/4$ cup ($1/2$ stick) butter
1 cup fresh blueberries or frozen
  unsweetened blueberries, partially thawed
1 cup sifted confectioners' sugar
1 teaspoon vanilla extract
1 teaspoon grated lemon zest
2 to 3 teaspoons lemon juice

Combine the egg, yogurt and 1 teaspoon lemon zest in a bowl and mix well. Combine the flour, granulated sugar, baking powder, baking soda and salt in a bowl and mix well. Cut in the butter with a pastry blender or fork until crumbly. Make a well in the center of the dry ingredients and pour in the egg mixture. Stir just until moistened. Fold in the blueberries.

Drop by rounded tablespoonfuls onto a greased baking sheet. Bake at 400 degrees for 15 to 18 minutes or until golden brown. Remove the biscuits to a wire rack.

Combine the confectioners' sugar, vanilla and 1 teaspoon lemon zest in a bowl. Stir in enough lemon juice to make a glaze. Drizzle over the warm biscuits. Serve immediately. *Serves 12.*

TWO WAYS TO MAKE FRENCH TOAST

IN THE OVEN

4 eggs
1/4 cup (1/2 stick) butter, melted
1 cup milk
1/2 teaspoon salt
8 thick slices firm white bread

ON THE GRIDDLE

4 eggs
1 cup milk
2 tablespoons Grand Marnier
1 tablespoon sugar
1/2 teaspoon vanilla extract
1/2 teaspoon salt
8 thick slices firm white bread
Confectioners' sugar

To bake in the oven, beat the eggs and melted butter in a bowl. Stir in the milk and salt. Pour into a flat shallow dish. Dip the bread slices in the egg mixture, coating each side. Arrange on a well-buttered baking sheet. Bake at 450 degrees for 8 minutes. Turn over the bread slices and bake for 5 minutes longer. *Serves 8.*

To cook on the griddle, beat the eggs, milk, liqueur, sugar, vanilla and salt in a bowl. Arrange the bread slices in a single layer in a baking dish.

Pour the egg mixture evenly over the bread. Turn over the bread slices. Chill, covered, overnight.

Heat and butter the griddle. Cook the bread until golden brown on both sides. Remove to serving plates and dust with confectioners' sugar. *Serves 8.*

Note: You may follow the griddle recipe and bake it in the oven, but add 1/4 cup melted butter to the egg mixture.

DELUXE PANCAKE MIX

3 cups whole wheat flour
1 cup (scant) unbleached all-purpose flour
1 cup buckwheat flour
1 cup cornmeal
1 cup wheat germ
3 tablespoons sugar
4 teaspoons baking powder
2$\frac{1}{2}$ teaspoons baking soda
2 teaspoons salt

Combine the whole wheat flour, all-purpose flour, buckwheat flour, cornmeal, wheat germ, sugar, baking powder, baking soda and salt in a bowl and mix well. Pour into a container with a tight-fitting lid and store in the refrigerator. ***Makes 7 cups.***

Note: To make pancakes, combine 1 cup Deluxe Pancake Mix, 1 cup milk, 1 egg and 2 tablespoons vegetable oil or melted butter in a bowl and mix lightly. Ladle onto a hot greased griddle or skillet and cook until golden brown on both sides. ***Serves 8.***

FAVORITE PANCAKE

$1/2$ cup all-purpose flour
$1/2$ cup milk
2 eggs, lightly beaten
Pinch of nutmeg
$1/4$ cup ($1/2$ stick) butter
2 tablespoons confectioners' sugar
Juice of $1/2$ lemon

Combine the flour, milk, eggs and nutmeg in a bowl and mix lightly. Melt the butter in a 12-inch ovenproof skillet in the oven. Tilt to coat the skillet evenly with melted butter. Pour the batter into the hot skillet.

Bake at 425 degrees for 15 to 20 minutes or until golden brown. Sprinkle with the confectioners' sugar and bake a few minutes longer. Sprinkle with the lemon juice and serve. ***Serves 2.***

CAKE THAT WON'T LAST

3 eggs, beaten
3 cups sugar
1 cup vegetable oil
1 (8-ounce) can crushed pineapple
1 teaspoon vanilla extract
3 cups sifted all-purpose flour

1 teaspoon baking soda
1 teaspoon salt
1 to 1^1/$_2$ teaspoons ground cinnamon
2 cups finely chopped bananas
1 cup chopped nuts

Combine the eggs, sugar, oil, pineapple and vanilla in a bowl and mix well. Add the flour, baking soda, salt and cinnamon and mix well; do not beat. Fold in the bananas and nuts. Pour into a well-greased bundt pan.

Bake at 350 degrees for 1 hour. Reduce the heat to 300 degrees and bake for 30 minutes longer or until the cake tests done. Cool in the pan for 15 minutes. Invert onto a serving plate. *Serves 16.*

CINNAMON PECAN COFFEE CAKE

2 cups all-purpose flour
1 teaspoon baking powder
1 teaspoon baking soda
^{1}/$_2$ teaspoon salt
^{1}/$_2$ cup (1 stick) butter, softened
1 cup granulated sugar
2 eggs

1 tablespoon vanilla extract
1 cup sour cream
^{1}/$_2$ cup granulated sugar
^{1}/$_3$ cup packed brown sugar
1 teaspoon ground cinnamon
1 cup chopped pecans

Sift the flour, baking powder, baking soda and salt together. Beat the butter, 1 cup granulated sugar, the eggs and vanilla in a bowl until light and fluffy. Stir in the dry ingredients alternately with the sour cream. Spread half the batter in a greased 9×13-inch baking pan. Combine ^{1}/$_2$ cup granulated sugar, the brown sugar, cinnamon and pecans in a bowl and mix well.

Sprinkle half the pecan mixture over the batter in the baking pan. Dollop the remaining batter over the pecan mixture. Sprinkle the remaining pecan mixture over the top of the batter.

Swirl a knife through the batter gently to create a marbled effect. Bake at 325 degrees for 40 to 45 minutes. Remove to a wire rack to cool. *Serves 15.*

SOUR CREAM ORANGE COFFEE CAKE

3 cups all-purpose flour
1^1/$_2$ teaspoons baking soda
1^1/$_2$ teaspoons baking powder
^{3}/$_4$ cup (1^1/$_2$ sticks) butter, softened
1^1/$_2$ cups granulated sugar
3 eggs
1^1/$_2$ teaspoons grated orange zest
1^1/$_2$ teaspoons vanilla extract

1^1/$_2$ cups sour cream
^{1}/$_4$ cup orange juice
1^1/$_2$ cups packed brown sugar
1 tablespoon ground cinnamon
6 tablespoons butter, softened
1^1/$_2$ cups chopped pecans
1 cup chocolate chips

Sift the flour, baking soda and baking powder together. Beat ^{3}/$_4$ cup butter and the granulated sugar in a bowl until light and fluffy. Add the eggs one at a time, beating well after each addition. Beat in the orange zest and vanilla. Beat in the dry ingredients alternately with the sour cream and orange juice. Spread half the batter in a greased 9×13-inch baking pan. Combine the brown sugar, cinnamon and 6 tablespoons butter in a bowl.

Mix the brown sugar mixture with your hands until crumbly. Add the pecans and chocolate chips and mix well. Sprinkle half the pecan mixture over the batter in the baking pan. Spread the remaining batter over the pecan mixture. Sprinkle the remaining pecan mixture over the top of the batter. Bake at 350 degrees for 30 minutes. Cover loosely with foil and bake for 35 minutes longer. Remove to a wire rack to cool. *Serves 15.*

BLUEBERRY BUCKLE

A favorite recipe from a past president

2 cups all-purpose flour
2 teaspoons baking powder
1/2 teaspoon salt
1/4 cup (1/2 stick) butter, softened
3/4 cup granulated sugar
1 egg

1/2 cup milk
2 cups fresh blueberries
1/2 cup packed brown sugar
1/3 cup all-purpose flour
11/2 teaspoons ground cinnamon
1/2 cup (1 stick) butter, softened

Sift 2 cups flour, the baking powder and salt together. Beat 1/4 cup butter, the granulated sugar and egg in a bowl until light and fluffy. Beat in the dry ingredients alternately with the milk. Fold in the blueberries. Spread in a greased 9×11-inch baking pan.

Combine the brown sugar, 1/3 cup flour, the cinnamon and 1/2 cup butter in a bowl and mix until crumbly. Sprinkle over the batter. Bake at 350 degrees for 40 minutes or until light brown. Remove to a wire rack to cool. *Serves 12.*

HOT CURRIED FRUIT

A favorite recipe from a past president

1 (29-ounce) can pear halves, drained
1 (29-ounce) can peach halves, drained
1 (20-ounce) can pineapple chunks, drained
2 (17-ounce) cans apricot halves, drained

1/2 cup (1 stick) butter, softened
1 cup packed brown sugar
1 tablespoon cornstarch
11/2 teaspoons curry powder

Spread the pears, peaches, pineapple and apricots over the bottom of a 9×13-inch baking dish. Combine the butter, brown sugar, cornstarch and curry powder in a bowl and mix well. Spoon over the fruit. Bake at 325 degrees for 1 hour, basting occasionally with the cooking liquid. *Serves 8 to 10.*

Note: The fruit can be cut into smaller pieces, if desired. This can be prepared up to 2 days ahead and chilled, covered, in the refrigerator. Baking time may need to be adjusted.

BREAKFAST COOKIES

2 cups rolled oats
1 1/4 cups whole wheat flour
1 cup all-purpose flour
1 cup Grape-Nuts cereal
1/2 cup wheat germ
1/2 cup oat bran
2 teaspoons baking soda
2 cups (4 sticks) unsalted butter, softened
2 eggs

1 cup packed light brown sugar
1/2 cup granulated sugar
1 tablespoon vanilla extract
1 cup (about 5 ounces) almonds, toasted and chopped
1 cup (about 5 ounces) raisins
1 cup (about 8 ounces) chopped pitted dates
14 pitted dates, cut into halves lengthwise

Combine the oats, whole wheat flour, all-purpose flour, cereal, wheat germ, oat bran and baking soda in a bowl and mix well. Beat the butter in a large bowl with an electric mixer until light and fluffy. Beat in the eggs, brown sugar, granulated sugar and vanilla. Add the dry ingredients and mix well. Stir in the almonds, raisins and chopped dates. Drop 1/4 cupfuls of dough 2 inches apart onto two baking parchment-lined baking sheets.

Flatten to 1/2-inch-thick mounds using damp fingers. Press one date half into the center of each cookie. Bake one sheet at a time at 350 degrees for 15 minutes or until light brown. Cool on the cookie sheet for 10 minutes. Remove to a wire rack to cool completely. *Serves 14.*

Note: These cookies freeze well.

GRANOLA

1 (18-ounce) package rolled oats
1 cup walnut pieces
3/4 cup vegetable oil
3/4 cup honey
1 teaspoon vanilla extract

1 teaspoon ground cinnamon
1 cup dried cranberries
1 cup golden raisins
1 cup currants

Combine the oats, walnuts, oil, honey, vanilla and cinnamon in a bowl and mix well. Spread over the bottom of two large baking pans. Bake at 300 degrees for 50 to 60 minutes or until brown. Let stand until cool. Stir in the dried cranberries, raisins and currants. *Makes 6 cups.*

Note: Use any dried fruits; apricots, dates, and cherries are also good. Serve as a breakfast cereal with milk or as a dessert with yogurt and fresh berries.

Beef Brisket 85
Oven-Roasted Beef Tenderloin 85
Roast Beef Tenderloin in a
   Dry Rub Crust 86
Monterey Lasagna 87
Golden Glow Pork Chops 87
Pork Tenderloin with Maple
   Mustard Sauce 88
Baked Pork Tenderloin
   with Mustard Sauce 89
Pork Loin Piccata 89
Curried Back of Pork Ribs 90
Smoked Sausage Gumbo 91
Spaghetti Pie 91
Penne with Sausage and Broccoli Rabe . . .92
Tuscan Pizza 93
Braised Lamb Shanks 94
Marinated Greek Butterflied Lamb 94
Rosemary-Marinated Lamb
   on the Grill .95
Tarragon Lemon Rack of Lamb 95

Loin of Venison with Mustard
   Pepper Marinade 96
Bengal Tigers 97
Cherry Chicken Jubilee 97
Quick-and-Easy Whiskey Chicken 98
Winter Chicken 98
Chicken Thighs Baked with Lemon,
   Sage, Rosemary and Thyme 99
Calypso Chicken 100
Hot Chicken Salad 100
Black Bean Chicken Chili 101
White Chili 101
Apple-Brined Turkey 102
Turkey Madras 102
Cornish Hens with
   Winter Fruit 103
Pheasant with Shotgun Sauce 103
Crab Cakes and Tartar Sauce 104
Grilled Halibut 104
Roasted Halibut with
   Fresh Herb Sauce 105

Garlicky Scallops and Shrimp 106
Linguini with Shrimp and
   Sun-Dried Tomatoes 106
Seafood Stew with Tomatoes,
   Shrimp and Scallops 107
Cod with Tomato and
   Artichoke Sauce 108
Oriental Grouper 108
One-Dish Salmon 109
Chilled Poached Salmon with Mustard
   Dill Sauce .110
Seared Roasted Salmon Fillets with
   Lemon Ginger Butter 110
Special Grilled Salmon 111
Spiced Salmon with Yellow Peppers 112
Hoisin-Glazed Sea Bass 113
Honey Soy Ahi Tuna Steaks 113
Bow Tie Pasta with Fresh Tomato
   Basil Sauce 114
Dry Rub for Beef, Pork or Poultry
   Barbecue 115

ENTRÉES

Entrées

The setting on the facing page was designed and the accessories were selected by Randy Forester of Studio 330, Bloomfield Hills, Michigan, and photographed by Yakov Faytlin in The Village Club library.

5

ENTRÉES

Entrées

THE LIBRARY OF THE VILLAGE CLUB CIRCA 1961
The sculptured ceiling, bookshelves, wood paneling, windows, and wall sconces of the
Winningham House library remain the same in the present-day Village Club. The library's
glowing fireplace and cozy atmosphere make it a favorite place for small gatherings—luncheons,
dinner parties, and meetings. It retains the warmth, comfort, and feeling of the past.

BEEF BRISKET

1 (3- to 5-pound) special-trim beef brisket
Salt and pepper to taste
Garlic powder to taste
1 large white onion or yellow onion, sliced
2 cups orange juice
1/4 cup packed brown sugar
1/4 cup ketchup

Season the brisket with salt, pepper and garlic powder. Place the brisket and onion in a roasting pan. Roast, uncovered, at 450 degrees for 20 minutes. Turn over the brisket. Roast, uncovered, for 20 minutes longer. Stir the onion, scraping any of the brown bits from the bottom of the pan.

Whisk the orange juice, brown sugar and ketchup in a bowl until mixed. Pour over the brisket. Reduce the oven temperature to 325 degrees.

Roast the brisket, covered, for 3 hours or until very tender, basting two or three times with the sauce. Remove to a serving plate and let stand for 20 minutes before slicing. Pour the onions and sauce into a saucepan and keep warm over low heat. *Serves 6 to 8.*

Note: You may add potatoes and carrots 1 hour before the end of the roasting time. Keep warm in a baking dish in the oven while preparing the brisket.

OVEN-ROASTED BEEF TENDERLOIN

1 (2-pound) beef tenderloin
1/4 cup chopped onion
2 tablespoons butter or margarine
1 teaspoon Dijon mustard
2 tablespoons soy sauce
Dash of pepper

Place the tenderloin on a wire rack in a shallow baking pan. Sauté the onion in the butter in a small saucepan until tender. Stir in the Dijon mustard, soy sauce and pepper.

Pour the onion mixture evenly over the tenderloin. Roast at 475 degrees for 15 minutes. Turn off the oven. Let the tenderloin stand in the closed oven for 45 minutes. *Serves 6 to 8.*

ROAST BEEF TENDERLOIN IN A DRY RUB CRUST

ROAST

1/4 cup olive oil
3 tablespoons thyme
3 tablespoons rosemary
2 tablespoons finely chopped garlic
3 tablespoons freshly ground pepper
2 tablespoons coarse salt
1 (5- to 6-pound) beef tenderloin, trimmed and tied
2 tablespoons olive oil

WINE SAUCE

1 cup red wine
2 tablespoons chopped shallots
Salt and pepper to taste
1 tablespoon chopped fresh thyme
1 tablespoon butter

For the roast, place a roasting pan in a 425-degree oven for 10 minutes. Combine 1/4 cup olive oil, the thyme, rosemary, garlic, pepper and coarse salt in a bowl and mix well. Rub evenly over the tenderloin. Drizzle 2 tablespoons olive oil over the bottom of the preheated roasting pan, tilting to coat the bottom. Place the tenderloin in the pan. Roast for 10 minutes. Turn over the tenderloin. Roast for 10 minutes longer. Reduce the oven temperature to 375 degrees. Roast for 15 to 18 minutes or to 135 degrees on a meat thermometer for medium-rare.

For the sauce, combine the wine, shallots, salt and pepper in a saucepan. Cook until reduced by half, stirring constantly. Whisk in the thyme and butter. Cook until heated through, stirring constantly.

Let the tenderloin stand for 15 to 20 minutes. Slice and arrange on a serving plate. Spoon the wine sauce evenly over the top. *Serves 8 to 10.*

Note: You may double the amount of sauce and add sautéed sliced mushrooms.

All hail the king, beef tenderloin—the king of beef—and his best friend
Cabernet Sauvignon. Cabernet Sauvignon just loves beef tenderloin:
Bordeaux, California, Chile, Australia, and Italian. The Stag's Leap or Oak Knoll
region pairs particularly well with tenderloin. Try Cabernet Sauvignon with Oven-Roasted
Beef Tenderloin (page 85) or Roast Beef Tenderloin in a Dry Rub Crust (above).

MONTEREY LASAGNA

1³/4 pounds lean ground beef
1/4 cup chopped green onions
1 envelope taco seasoning mix
1 cup water
1 (8-ounce) can tomato sauce
1/2 cup tomato paste
2 cups light sour cream

1 egg, lightly beaten
1/2 cup sliced black olives
10 to 12 flour tortillas, cut into halves
2 cups (8 ounces) shredded sharp Cheddar cheese
2 cups (8 ounces) shredded Monterey Jack cheese
1/2 cup mild or medium green chiles, chopped

Brown the ground beef with the green onions in a large skillet, stirring until the ground beef is crumbly; drain. Stir in the seasoning mix and water. Simmer for 5 minutes. Stir in the tomato sauce and tomato paste. Simmer for 3 to 4 minutes or until slightly thickened. Remove from the heat. Combine the sour cream, egg and olives in a bowl and mix well. Spread enough of the ground beef mixture in a 9×13-inch baking dish to lightly cover the bottom. Arrange one-third of the tortillas over the ground beef layer, overlapping the tortillas slightly. Cover with half the remaining ground beef mixture and spread with half the sour cream mixture.

Sprinkle with one-third of the Cheddar cheese and one-third of the Monterey Jack cheese. Continue layering with half the remaining tortillas, the remaining ground beef mixture, the remaining sour cream mixture, half the remaining Cheddar cheese, half the remaining Monterey Jack cheese and the chiles. Top with the remaining tortillas and sprinkle with the remaining Cheddar cheese and Monterey Jack cheese. Bake at 350 degrees for 30 to 35 minutes or until bubbly and light brown. Let stand for 5 minutes before serving. Serve with chopped tomatoes, avocado slices, taco sauce and sour cream, if desired. *Serves 6 to 8.*

GOLDEN GLOW PORK CHOPS

5 or 6 pork chops
Salt and pepper to taste
1 (29-ounce) can cling peach halves, drained, 1/4 cup juice reserved
1/4 cup packed brown sugar

1/2 teaspoon ground cinnamon
1/4 teaspoon ground cloves
1 (8-ounce) can tomato sauce
1/4 cup vinegar

Brown the pork chops lightly on both sides in a nonstick skillet. Remove to a slow cooker and season with salt and pepper. Place the peach halves over the pork chops. Drain excess drippings from the skillet.

Add the remaining ingredients to the skillet. Bring to a boil, stirring frequently. Pour evenly over the pork chops. Cook on Low for 4 to 6 hours or until the pork chops are cooked through and tender. *Serves 5 or 6.*

PORK TENDERLOIN WITH MAPLE MUSTARD SAUCE

¹/2 teaspoon nutmeg
¹/2 teaspoon thyme, crushed
¹/2 teaspoon garlic salt
¹/4 teaspoon basil, crushed
¹/4 teaspoon ground cloves
¹/4 teaspoon ground cinnamon
¹/8 teaspoon ground allspice

¹/4 teaspoon black pepper
¹/4 teaspoon cayenne pepper
1 (1-pound) pork tenderloin
3 bay leaves
2 tablespoons olive oil
²/3 cup maple syrup
¹/4 cup Dijon mustard

Combine the nutmeg, thyme, garlic salt, basil, cloves, cinnamon, allspice, black pepper and cayenne pepper in a bowl and mix well. Rub evenly over the tenderloin. Place the bay leaves under the tenderloin on a piece of plastic wrap. Seal the tenderloin in the plastic wrap and chill for at least 2 hours. Unwrap the tenderloin and place on a rack in a shallow roasting pan.

Brush the tenderloin with the olive oil. Roast at 425 degrees for 30 to 35 minutes or to 160 to 170 degrees on a meat thermometer. Remove the tenderloin to a cutting board and discard the bay leaves. Whisk the maple syrup and Dijon mustard in a bowl. Slice the pork diagonally and arrange on a serving plate. Serve with the maple mustard sauce. *Serves 4.*

Sweet and aromatic pork performs great with big but gentle wines. The wines of Rioja are based on the Tempnillo grape, nicknamed "the gentle giant." Try the producers Lan, Marques de Casersce, or Muga. They are best four to seven years after vintage date. Decant for a half hour to mellow the gamy nature of Rioja. Roija wines pair especially well with Pork Tenderloin with Maple Mustard Sauce (above) and Golden Glow Pork Chops (page 87).

BAKED PORK TENDERLOIN WITH MUSTARD SAUCE

A Village Club favorite from **Food With A Flair**

MUSTARD SAUCE
1/3 cup each sour cream and mayonnaise
1 teaspoon dry mustard
1 teaspoon finely chopped shallots
11/2 teaspoons vinegar
Salt to taste

PORK
1/4 cup soy sauce
1/4 cup bourbon
2 tablespoons brown sugar
1 pork tenderloin

For the sauce, combine the sour cream and mayonnaise in a bowl and mix well. Stir in the dry mustard, shallots, vinegar and salt.

For the pork, combine the soy sauce, bourbon and brown sugar in a bowl and mix well. Pour over the tenderloin in a shallow dish; cover.

Chill for several hours, turning two or three times. Remove to a baking dish, reserving the marinade. Bake at 325 degrees for 1 hour or to 165 degrees on a meat thermometer, basting often with the reserved marinade. Discard any remaining marinade. Cut the tenderloin diagonally into thin slices. Serve with the sauce. *Serves 2.*

PORK LOIN PICCATA

1/3 cup all-purpose flour
2 tablespoons cornmeal
1/2 teaspoon salt
1/2 teaspoon white pepper
1 tablespoon each margarine and vegetable oil
2 or 3 garlic cloves, minced

12 thin boneless pork loin slices or medallions
6 to 12 very thin lemon slices
Seasoned salt to taste
1 tablespoon capers
1/4 cup finely chopped fresh parsley
1 cup (about) dry white wine

Mix the flour, cornmeal, salt and white pepper in a shallow dish. Heat one-third each of the margarine, oil and garlic in a skillet until hot.

Coat four of the pork slices with the flour mixture and add to the skillet. Sauté the pork until light brown. Remove to a shallow baking dish, overlapping the slices slightly. Repeat two times, using the remaining margarine, oil, garlic and pork.

Place half or one slice of lemon on each pork slice. Sprinkle with seasoned salt and top with the capers and parsley. Pour the wine into the baking dish to a depth of 1/4 inch. Bake, covered, at 350 degrees for 20 to 30 minutes or until the pork is cooked through. *Serves 6.*

Note: You may use veal scallops or pounded boneless chicken breasts instead of pork.

CURRIED BACK OF PORK RIBS

<table>
<tr><td>2 tablespoons butter</td><td>2 teaspoons all-purpose flour</td></tr>
<tr><td>1/2 cup chopped onion</td><td>1/4 cup heavy cream</td></tr>
<tr><td>1 teaspoon curry powder</td><td>1/2 cup chicken broth</td></tr>
<tr><td>1/2 teaspoon salt</td><td>3 pounds pork spareribs</td></tr>
<tr><td>1/4 teaspoon celery salt</td><td>1/4 cup heavy cream</td></tr>
<tr><td>1/4 teaspoon thyme</td><td>1/2 cup chicken broth</td></tr>
<tr><td>1/4 teaspoon white pepper</td><td>1 cup rice</td></tr>
</table>

Melt the butter in a saucepan. Add the onion, curry powder, salt, celery salt, thyme and white pepper and sauté for 5 minutes. Stir in the flour. Stir in 1/4 cup cream and 1/2 cup broth.

Arrange the ribs in a shallow baking pan. Bake at 325 degrees for 1 to 11/2 hours.

Spoon half the sauce over the ribs. Bake for 30 minutes or until the pork is cooked through.

Combine the remaining sauce, 1/4 cup cream and 1/2 cup broth in a bowl and mix well. Pour over the rice in a baking dish. Bake, covered, at 325 degrees for 30 minutes or until the rice is tender. *Serves 4 to 6.*

*T*he curry in the Curried Back of Pork Ribs (above) is an aggressive flavor and likes to be paired with an aggressive wine. A big Aussie Shiraz will fit the bill. Look to the Barossa Valley. Torbeck and Peter Lehman are outstanding producers, and both offer great wines in every price range. Let both of these producers' wines breathe for at least an hour to help with the curry integration.

SMOKED SAUSAGE GUMBO

1 (14-ounce) can diced tomatoes
1 cup chicken broth
1/4 cup all-purpose flour
2 tablespoons olive oil
12 ounces Polish sausage, cut into 1/2-inch pieces
1 onion, chopped
1 green bell pepper, chopped

2 ribs celery, chopped
1 carrot, chopped
2 teaspoons oregano
2 teaspoons thyme
1/8 teaspoon cayenne pepper
3 cups hot cooked rice

Mix the tomatoes and broth in a slow cooker. Sprinkle the flour over the bottom of a small skillet. Cook over high heat for 3 to 4 minutes or until the flour begins to brown; do not stir. Reduce the heat to medium and cook for 4 minutes, stirring constantly. Stir in the olive oil. Cook until smooth, stirring constantly.

Whisk the flour mixture carefully into the tomato mixture in the slow cooker. Add the sausage, onion, bell pepper, celery, carrot, oregano, thyme and cayenne pepper and mix well. Cook on Low for 41/2 to 5 hours or until the sausage is cooked through and the liquid is thickened. Serve over the rice. *Serves 4.*

SPAGHETTI PIE

1 (6-ounce) package thin spaghetti or vermicelli, cooked al dente, drained and chopped
1/2 garlic clove, minced
1/4 cup (1/2 stick) butter, softened
11/2 cups (6 ounces) shredded Parmesan cheese
1 egg, beaten
1 tablespoon chopped fresh basil, or
1 teaspoon dried basil
1 cup ricotta cheese or sour cream

12 ounces bulk Italian sausage
8 ounces ground beef
1/2 cup chopped onion
1 (15-ounce) can tomato sauce
1 (6-ounce) can tomato paste
1 teaspoon sugar
1 teaspoon each dried basil and oregano
1/4 cup white wine
6 ounces mozzarella cheese, shredded

Combine the spaghetti, garlic, butter, Parmesan cheese, egg and fresh basil in a bowl and mix well. Press over the bottom and up the side of a 10-inch deep-dish pie plate. Spread the ricotta cheese over the pasta crust. Brown the sausage and ground beef with the onion in a skillet, stirring until the ground beef and sausage are crumbly; drain.

Stir in the tomato sauce, tomato paste, sugar, dried basil, oregano and wine. Cook until heated through. Spoon over the ricotta cheese in the pie plate.

Sprinkle the mozzarella cheese over the pie. Bake at 350 degrees for 30 minutes. This pie freezes well. *Serves 6 to 8.*

PENNE WITH SAUSAGE AND BROCCOLI RABE

3 garlic cloves, quartered
3 tablespoons extra-virgin olive oil
Coarse salt to taste
1 bunch broccoli rabe, trimmed (about 1 pound)
1/4 cup extra-virgin olive oil
1 pound sweet Italian sausage with fennel, casings removed and sausage cut into 1/2-inch pieces

1 (7-ounce) jar oil-pack sun-dried tomatoes, drained and cut into small pieces
12 plum tomatoes, seeded and quartered
4 garlic cloves, crushed
1/4 teaspoon crushed red pepper flakes
16 ounces penne pasta, cooked al dente and drained
Salt and freshly ground black pepper to taste

Place the quartered garlic cloves on a square of foil. Drizzle with 3 tablespoons olive oil and season with coarse salt. Seal the garlic in the foil and place on a baking sheet. Bake at 350 degrees for 15 minutes or until golden brown and softened.

Cook the broccoli rabe in a large pot of boiling water for 1 to 2 minutes or until bright green. Drain and cut the broccoli rabe crosswise into 1-inch pieces. Heat 1/4 cup olive oil in a large skillet over medium heat for 1 to 2 minutes or until fragrant.

Add the sausage and sauté for 10 minutes or until cooked through; drain. Stir in the broccoli rabe, sun-dried tomatoes, plum tomatoes, crushed garlic cloves and red pepper flakes. Sauté for 2 to 3 minutes. Toss the pasta with the quartered garlic mixture in a bowl. Stir into the sausage mixture and season with salt and pepper. *Serves 4 to 6.*

Note: You may use 4 cups canned tomatoes, quartered, instead of plum tomatoes.

One of the best grapes for pasta—whether with a plain tomato sauce or a puttanesca sauce—is the Nero D'Avola from Sicily. The Nero D'Avola is delicious in both its light and its heavy forms. The Arancio is the lighter style, and Cusumano is the heavier style. Try either style with the Penne with Sausage and Broccoli Rabe (above).

TUSCAN PIZZA

3¹/2 cups all-purpose flour
³/4 cup (1¹/2 sticks) cold
    unsalted butter
¹/4 cup cold shortening
1 teaspoon salt
3 eggs, beaten
2 to 4 tablespoons ice water
1 tablespoon olive oil
8 ounces bulk hot Italian sausage
1 tablespoon olive oil

2 (12-ounce) packages fresh spinach,
    stems removed, coarsely chopped
4 egg yolks, lightly beaten
2 cups ricotta cheese
12 ounces mozzarella cheese, shredded
¹/3 cup freshly grated Parmesan cheese
¹/2 cup chopped pepperoni
1 egg, beaten
2 tablespoons freshly grated
    Parmesan cheese

Combine the flour, butter, shortening and salt in a food processor and process until the mixture resembles coarse crumbs. Add three eggs and pulse to blend. Add the ice water 1 tablespoonful at a time, processing constantly until the dough forms a ball. Divide the dough into two disks, one being twice the size of the other. Wrap the disks in plastic wrap and chill for 30 minutes. Heat 1 tablespoon olive oil in a large skillet over medium heat. Add the sausage and sauté for 5 minutes or until the sausage is cooked through; drain. Remove the sausage to a bowl. Add 1 tablespoon olive oil to the skillet and heat over medium heat. Add the spinach and sauté for 10 minutes or until the spinach is wilted and the juices have evaporated.

Combine the egg yolks, ricotta cheese, mozzarella cheese and ¹/3 cup Parmesan cheese in a bowl and mix well. Stir in the sausage, spinach and pepperoni. Roll the larger disk of dough into a 17-inch circle on a floured surface. Fit into a 9-inch springform pan, trimming the dough to overhang the pan by 1 inch. Spoon the sausage mixture into the prepared pan. Roll the remaining dough into a 12-inch circle. Place over the filling and pinch the edge to seal. Brush the top with 1 beaten egg and sprinkle with 2 tablespoons Parmesan cheese. Bake at 375 degrees on the bottom oven rack for 1 hour. *Serves 8.*

Note: You may use one 10-ounce package frozen leaf spinach, thawed, instead of fresh spinach.

BRAISED LAMB SHANKS

8 lamb shanks
All-purpose flour
1/4 cup vegetable oil
1 onion, sliced
4 garlic cloves, minced
1 cup ketchup

1 cup water
2 tablespoons Worcestershire sauce
1/2 cup cider vinegar
1/4 cup packed brown sugar
2 teaspoons dry mustard
1 cup raisins

Coat the lamb with flour. Heat the oil in a large Dutch oven on the stovetop. Add the lamb and brown on all sides. Drain off any excess oil. Place the onion over the lamb shanks. Combine the garlic, ketchup, water, Worcestershire sauce, vinegar, brown sugar, dry mustard and raisins in a saucepan and mix well. Cook until heated through, stirring frequently.

Pour over the lamb and onion. Bake, covered, at 350 degrees for 2 hours or until the lamb is tender. Baste the lamb with the sauce. Bake, uncovered, for 15 minutes longer. *Serves 8.*

Note: This recipe can be made 1 day ahead. Chill, covered, in the refrigerator. This also freezes well.

MARINATED GREEK BUTTERFLIED LAMB

2/3 cup (about) olive oil
41/2 teaspoons soy sauce
1 onion, chopped
Juice of 1 lemon
2 garlic cloves, chopped
Dash of Tabasco sauce
1 teaspoon salt

1/4 teaspoon thyme
1/4 teaspoon marjoram
1/4 teaspoon oregano
1 bay leaf
1/4 cup chopped fresh parsley
1/4 teaspoon Worcestershire sauce
1 (5-pound) butterflied leg of lamb

Combine the olive oil, soy sauce, onion, lemon juice, garlic, Tabasco sauce, salt, thyme, marjoram, oregano, bay leaf, parsley and Worcestershire sauce in a food processor. Pulse until coarsely chopped. Spread the marinade over the lamb in a baking dish. Chill, covered, for at least 3 hours, turning the lamb occasionally.

Bake, uncovered, at 375 degrees for 20 to 25 minutes or to 120 degrees on a meat thermometer. Remove the lamb to a rack in a broiler pan. Broil for 2 to 3 minutes or until light brown. Let stand for 8 to 10 minutes before carving. *Serves 10.*

ROSEMARY-MARINATED LAMB ON THE GRILL

A favorite recipe from a past president

1 cup olive oil
1/2 cup Dijon mustard
1 tablespoon dry mustard
15 garlic cloves, crushed
1 1/2 cups fresh rosemary sprigs
2 teaspoons salt

1/4 cup lemon juice, or the juice of
  2 to 3 lemons
1/2 teaspoon cayenne pepper, or
  5 or 6 dried red chiles, crushed
Black pepper to taste
1 butterflied leg of lamb

Combine the olive oil, Dijon mustard, dry mustard, garlic, rosemary, salt, lemon juice, cayenne pepper and black pepper in a bowl and mix well. Pour over the lamb in a baking dish. Chill, covered, for 2 to 3 days, turning the lamb daily.

Discard the marinade. Grill the lamb for 15 to 20 minutes per side or to desired doneness. *Serves 8 to 10.*

Note: This can also be baked in the marinade in the oven. Stir in 1 to 1 1/2 cups white wine before baking.

TARRAGON LEMON RACK OF LAMB

2 (1 1/4-pound) trimmed and frenched
  single rack of lamb (14 to 16 ribs)
Salt and pepper to taste
2 tablespoons unsalted butter

2 teaspoons grated lemon zest
2 tablespoons fresh lemon juice
3/4 teaspoon dried tarragon, or
  4 teaspoons chopped fresh tarragon

Season the lamb with salt and pepper. Heat an ovenproof skillet over medium-high heat until hot. Add the lamb and cook for 4 minutes or until browned on all sides.

Drain excess drippings from the skillet. Arrange the lamb meat side up in the skillet. Roast at 475 degrees for 15 minutes or to 130 degrees on a meat thermometer for medium-rare.

Remove the lamb to a cutting board and let stand, uncovered, for 10 minutes. Melt the butter in a saucepan. Stir in the lemon zest, lemon juice and tarragon. Season with salt and pepper. Cut the lamb between the ribs and garnish with tarragon sprigs. Serve the sauce on the side. *Serves 4.*

Note: This recipe also works well with leg of lamb.

LOIN OF VENISON WITH MUSTARD PEPPER MARINADE

1/2 cup red wine
2 tablespoons whole grain mustard
1 (1 1/4-pound) venison loin
2 tablespoons cracked pepper
2 tablespoons ground juniper berries
2 teaspoons light olive oil

1/2 cup game stock or beef broth
2 tablespoons raspberry jam
1 cup fresh blueberries or frozen
  blueberries, thawed
Coarse salt (optional)

Pour the wine into a large nonreactive dish and stir in the mustard. Pat the venison dry. Mix the pepper and juniper berries in a bowl. Rub generously over the venison. Add the venison to the wine mixture and turn to coat all sides. Chill for 1 to 3 hours. Remove the venison from the marinade and pat dry. Discard the marinade. Cook the venison in the olive oil in a skillet over medium heat for 4 minutes or until all sides are brown and the venison is red to pink in the center.

Remove the venison from the skillet and wrap tightly in foil. Let stand for at least 10 minutes.

Add the stock to the skillet. Cook over high heat until the stock is reduced by half, scraping any brown bits from the bottom of the skillet. Stir in the jam and blueberries. Season with coarse salt, if desired. Cut the venison into 1/2-inch medallions and serve with the sauce. *Serves 4.*

*W*ild game is one of the toughest matches for a sommelier. One looks to control the gaminess without making the meat bland or losing the flavor that makes wild game unique. Châteaunuef-du-Pape, from producers like Paegue and Veaux Telegraph that are Grenache-based, really tempers the gaminess of venison without destroying the richness of the meat. Serve Châteaunuef-du-Pape with Loin of Venison with Mustard Pepper Marinade (above).

BENGAL TIGERS

Top favorite of Village Club members from **Food With A Flair**

4 whole chicken breasts, boned and split
Butter
1 (10-ounce) can cream of chicken soup
1 cup mayonnaise

1 tablespoon lemon juice
1 teaspoon curry powder
1/2 cup (2 ounces) shredded Cheddar cheese
1/2 cup herb-seasoned stuffing mix

Arrange the chicken in an 8×12-inch baking dish. Dot each chicken breast with a small piece of butter. Combine the soup, mayonnaise, lemon juice, curry powder and cheese in a bowl and mix well. Spread over the chicken. Sprinkle with the stuffing mix and dot with butter.

Bake at 300 degrees for 1 1/2 hours or until the chicken is cooked through. *Serves 4 to 6.*

Note: This can be prepared 1 day ahead. Chill, covered, in the refrigerator. Baking time may need to be adjusted.

CHERRY CHICKEN JUBILEE

All-purpose flour
Salt and pepper to taste
8 chicken breasts
1 onion, chopped
1/4 cup packed brown sugar

1/4 cup raisins
1/2 cup ketchup
1 tablespoon Worcestershire sauce
1/2 to 3/4 cup sliced mushrooms
1 can Bing cherries, drained, juice reserved

Season the flour with salt and pepper. Coat the chicken with flour. Brown the chicken on both sides in a nonstick skillet. Arrange in a buttered 9×13-inch baking pan.

Sauté the onion in a nonstick skillet until tender and golden brown. Stir in the brown sugar, raisins, ketchup, Worcestershire sauce and mushrooms.

Combine a small amount of the reserved cherry juice with enough water in a measuring cup to measure 1/4 to 1/2 cup liquid. Stir into the onion mixture. Pour evenly over the chicken. Bake, covered, at 350 degrees for 55 minutes or until the chicken is cooked through. Top with the cherries and bake, uncovered, for 5 minutes longer. *Serves 8.*

QUICK-AND-EASY WHISKEY CHICKEN

6 tablespoons butter
2 large boneless skinless chicken breasts
6 tablespoons bourbon
1^1/$_2$ teaspoons salt
^{1}/$_4$ teaspoon white pepper

8 ounces (or more) white mushrooms, thinly sliced
2 cups crème fraîche, sour cream or heavy cream
2 teaspoons beurre manié (1 teaspoon softened butter mixed with 1 teaspoon all-purpose flour)

Melt the butter in a skillet. Add the chicken and sauté for 4 to 5 minutes per side or until golden brown. Add the bourbon. Cook, covered, over low heat for 10 minutes. Stir in the salt, white pepper, mushrooms and crème fraîche. Bring to a boil.

Remove the chicken to a warm plate. Boil the mushroom mixture for 5 minutes. Stir in the beurre manié. Cook for 3 minutes, stirring constantly. Return the chicken to the sauce and cook until heated through. *Serves 4.*

WINTER CHICKEN

2 (2^1/$_2$- to 3-pound) chickens, each cut into 8 pieces
6 large garlic cloves, minced
2 tablespoons dried thyme
1 tablespoon cumin
1 teaspoon ginger
1 teaspoon salt
^{1}/$_2$ cup red wine vinegar

^{1}/$_2$ cup good-quality olive oil
1 cup imported black olives
1^1/$_2$ cups dried apricots
1 cup small dried figs or large fig pieces
^{1}/$_4$ cup packed brown sugar
^{1}/$_2$ cup madeira
1 cup large pecan pieces
Grated zest of 2 lemons

Combine the chicken, garlic, thyme, cumin, ginger, salt, vinegar, olive oil, olives, apricots and figs in a large bowl and mix well. Chill, covered, overnight. Let stand at room temperature for 1 hour before baking. Arrange the chicken in a single layer in a large baking pan. Spoon the marinade evenly over the chicken. Sprinkle with the brown sugar and pour the madiera between the chicken pieces. Bake, covered, at 350 degrees for 20 minutes.

Bake, uncovered, for 40 to 50 minutes longer or until the chicken is cooked through, basting frequently with the pan juices.

Remove the chicken, olives, apricots and figs to a large serving platter using a slotted spoon. Drizzle with a few large spoonfuls of the pan juices. Sprinkle with the pecans and lemon zest. Pour the remaining pan juices into a sauceboat and serve with the chicken. *Serves 6.*

CHICKEN THIGHS BAKED WITH LEMON, SAGE, ROSEMARY AND THYME

2 large garlic cloves
Kosher salt or sea salt
3 to 4 tablespoons extra-virgin olive oil
12 chicken thighs, trimmed, rinsed and patted dry
12 (1/4-inch) lemon slices
12 (2-inch) fresh rosemary sprigs
12 (2-inch) fresh thyme sprigs
12 fresh sage leaves
Freshly ground pepper

Mash the garlic with a pinch of salt into a thick paste using a mortar and pestle. Add the olive oil one drop at a time, mashing into a thick and creamy paste. Place the chicken in a bowl. Rub the paste all over the chicken, including under the skin. Chill, covered, for 2 hours to overnight. Arrange the lemon slices in a single layer in a shallow baking pan.

Top each slice with a sprig of rosemary, a sprig of thyme and a sage leaf. Place the chicken skin side up on top of the sage. Sprinkle generously with salt and pepper. Bake at 425 degrees on the middle oven rack for 45 minutes to 1 hour or until the chicken is golden brown and the juices run clear when pricked with a fork. *Serves 12.*

*V*ernaccia di San Gimignano is the first white wine to be assigned D.O.C.G. (highest level of Italian wine) status. It is considered the quintessential Italian white wine. It cuts oil and brings out rosemary and citrus flavors. The Falchini family makes a couple of great ones. Vernaccia pairs well with Chicken Thighs Baked with Lemon, Sage, Rosemary and Thyme (above).

CALYPSO CHICKEN

4¹/₂ teaspoons vegetable oil
2 boneless skinless chicken breasts,
cut into 1-inch pieces and patted dry
Salt and freshly ground pepper to taste
1 large onion, chopped
4^1/$_2$ teaspoons minced fresh ginger
1 zucchini, cut into ^{3}/$_8$-inch slices

1 sweet potato, peeled and cut into
^{3}/$_4$-inch pieces
1 small red bell pepper, cut into ^{3}/$_4$-inch pieces
1 large garlic clove, minced
1 cup chicken stock
1 to 2 tablespoons dark rum (optional)
^{1}/$_2$ cup orange marmalade or apricot marmalade

Heat the oil in a large wok over medium-high heat. Add the chicken and stir-fry for 2 to 3 minutes or until golden brown. Remove the chicken with a slotted spoon to a plate and season with salt and pepper. Add the onion, ginger, zucchini, sweet potato and bell pepper to the wok. Cook for 4 minutes or until the onion is tender and light brown, stirring frequently.

Stir in the garlic. Add the stock, rum and marmalade and mix well. Bring to a boil over high heat. Boil for 10 minutes.

Add the chicken. Cook for 5 minutes or until the chicken is cooked through. Season with salt and pepper. Garnish with thinly sliced scallions and toasted coconut, if desired. *Serves 2.*

HOT CHICKEN SALAD

A Village Club favorite from Food With A Flair

1 cup crushed potato chips
3 cups chopped cooked chicken (1-inch pieces)
2 cups chopped celery
1 cup mayonnaise
^{1}/$_2$ cup toasted almonds
2 tablespoons lemon juice

2 teaspoons grated onion
^{1}/$_2$ teaspoon salt
^{1}/$_4$ teaspoon celery seeds
^{1}/$_2$ cup (2 ounces) shredded cheese
1 cup crushed potato chips

Spread 1 cup potato chips over the bottom of an ungreased baking dish. Combine the chicken, celery, mayonnaise, almonds, lemon juice, onion, salt and celery seeds in a bowl and mix well. Spoon into the baking dish. Top with the cheese and 1 cup potato chips. Bake at 375 degrees for 20 minutes; do not overcook. *Serves 6.*

Note: You may add small amounts of diced pimento, chopped green bell pepper, ^{1}/$_2$ cup sliced mushrooms or ^{1}/$_2$ cup sliced water chestnuts, if desired. You may also use crab meat instead of chicken.

BLACK BEAN CHICKEN CHILI

3 boneless skinless chicken breasts
$1/4$ cup all-purpose flour
2 teaspoons olive oil
$4^1/2$ cups chicken broth
3 (15-ounce) cans black beans,
   drained and rinsed
$1/2$ red bell pepper, chopped
$1/2$ green bell pepper, chopped

$1/2$ yellow bell pepper, chopped
1 small onion, chopped
$1/2$ teaspoon salt
$1^1/2$ teaspoons freshly ground pepper
$1^1/2$ teaspoons smoked paprika or sweet paprika
1 tablespoon (or more) chili powder
1 tablespoon cumin
Dash of cayenne pepper (optional)

Coat the chicken with the flour. Heat the olive oil in an ovenproof skillet. Add the chicken and cook for 2 minutes. Turn over the chicken and cook for 2 minutes. Bake at 375 degrees for exactly 8 minutes. Remove the chicken to a cutting board and let cool slightly. Chop the chicken. Combine the remaining ingredients in a large saucepan and mix well. Stir in the chopped chicken. Bring to a boil and cook for 30 minutes, stirring occasionally.

Reduce the heat and simmer for 1 hour, stirring occasionally. *Serves 8.*

Note: Three cups of chopped purchased rotisserie chicken can be used instead of the chicken breasts. To make a thicker chili, remove 2 cups of chili to a blender and purée before returning to the saucepan.

WHITE CHILI

2 pounds boneless skinless chicken breasts
5 to 6 cups chicken broth
1 tablespoon olive oil
2 cups finely chopped onions
2 tablespoons minced garlic
2 jalapeño chiles, seeded and chopped

4 (16-ounce) cans Great Northern beans
$1/2$ cup chopped fresh cilantro
1 tablespoon each cumin and chopped fresh oregano
$1/4$ teaspoon cayenne pepper
2 to 3 dashes of Tabasco sauce
Salt to taste

Combine the chicken and enough of the broth to cover in a saucepan. Bring to a boil and reduce the heat. Simmer for 10 minutes. Remove the chicken to a cutting board and reserve the broth. Chop the chicken. Heat the olive oil in a large saucepan. Add the onions and garlic and sauté until tender.

Add the jalapeños and sauté for 1 to 2 minutes. Stir in the chopped chicken, reserved broth and remaining ingredients. Simmer for 30 minutes. *Serves 6 to 8.*

Note: This chili is best if made 1 day ahead. Chill, covered, in the refrigerator. Reheat before serving.

APPLE-BRINED TURKEY

8 cups apple juice
1 (16-ounce) package brown sugar
1 cup kosher salt
12 cups water
3 oranges, quartered
4 ounces fresh ginger, thinly sliced

15 whole cloves
6 bay leaves
6 garlic cloves, crushed
1 (12- to 14-pound turkey), rinsed and
  patted dry
Vegetable oil

Combine the apple juice, brown sugar and salt in a saucepan. Bring to a boil and boil for 1 minute, stirring constantly. Skim off the foam and let cool to room temperature. Mix the apple juice mixture, water, oranges, ginger, cloves, bay leaves and garlic in a 5-gallon food-grade plastic container. Submerge the turkey carefully into the brine. Add a weight, if necessary, to keep the turkey submerged.

Chill, covered, for 24 hours. Remove the turkey and discard the brine. Pat the turkey very dry. Brush oil lightly over the turkey. Roast or grill the turkey until the thigh meat reaches 180 degrees on a meat thermometer. *Serves 12 to 14.*

Note: A turkey breast may be used instead of a whole turkey but brine for a shorter time.

TURKEY MADRAS

1/2 cup golden raisins
3 tablespoons butter
3/4 cup chopped celery
3/4 cup chopped onion
4 large mushrooms, chopped
1 garlic clove, crushed
1 to 3 tablespoons curry powder, or to taste

1/4 cup all-purpose flour
1 tablespoon tomato paste
2 cups hot chicken broth
1 cup heavy cream
3 cups chopped cooked turkey
Salt and pepper to taste
Hot cooked rice

Plump the raisins in boiling water in a small bowl. Melt the butter in a large heavy saucepan. Add the celery, onion, mushrooms and garlic and sauté until the vegetables are tender. Add the curry powder, flour and tomato paste and stir with a wooden spoon. Cook for a few minutes, stirring constantly. Add the hot broth all at once and whisk well. Reduce the heat to low.

Simmer the mixture for 45 minutes. Drain the raisins and add to the saucepan. Stir in the cream, turkey, salt and pepper. Bring to a boil slowly, stirring frequently. Serve over rice and garnish with chutney, chopped hard-cooked egg, chopped peanuts or toasted almonds, flaked coconut, chopped cucumber or chopped onion, if desired. *Serves 6.*

CORNISH HENS WITH WINTER FRUIT

12 large garlic cloves
1 tablespoon oregano
Salt and pepper to taste
1 cup red wine vinegar
1/2 cup olive oil
1 cup pitted prunes or figs
1 cup dried apricots

1 cup pitted green olives or black olives
1/2 cup capers with a small amount of liquid
8 bay leaves
8 Cornish game hens, split, rinsed and patted dry
1 cup dry white wine or madeira
1 cup packed brown sugar

Combine the garlic, oregano, salt, pepper, vinegar, olive oil, prunes, apricots, olives, capers and bay leaves in a bowl and mix well. Pour over the game hens in a large bowl. Chill, covered, overnight. Arrange the game hens in a roasting pan and add the marinade. Add the white wine and sprinkle with the brown sugar. Bake at 350 degrees for 1 to 1 1/2 hours or until the game hens are cooked through, basting frequently with the pan juices.

Remove the game hens, prunes, apricots, olives and garlic cloves to a large serving platter using a slotted spoon. Remove and discard the bay leaves.

Pour the remaining pan juices into a sauceboat and serve separately. Serve with cooked wild rice or a combination of wild and white rice and sprinkle with chopped fresh parsley. *Serves 16.*

PHEASANT WITH SHOTGUN SAUCE

1/2 cup (1 stick) butter
1 cup currant jelly
1/2 teaspoon Worcestershire sauce
2 pheasants, split lengthwise
Salt and pepper to taste

3 slices bacon
1 tablespoon butter
2 tablespoons currant jelly
2 thick onion slices

Combine 1/2 cup butter, 1 cup currant jelly and the Worcestershire sauce in a saucepan. Bring to a boil. Cook for 5 minutes, stirring occasionally. Remove from the heat and skim the foam as it cools.

Season the cavity of each bird with salt and pepper. Place half a slice of bacon on each of two large pieces of foil. Place one bird half cavity side up on the bacon. Place 1/2 tablespoon butter and 1 tablespoon jelly in each cavity.

Top each with an onion slice and half a slice of bacon. Top with the remaining bird halves cavity side down to make two whole birds. Place half a slice of bacon on top of each bird. Seal the foil tightly around the birds and place on a baking sheet. Bake at 350 degrees for 3 hours. Remove the birds from the foil to a shallow roasting pan. Pour the sauce over the birds. Broil until light brown. *Serves 4.*

CRAB CAKES AND TARTAR SAUCE

TARTAR SAUCE

1 cup mayonnaise
2 tablespoons fresh lemon juice
1 teaspoon Worcestershire sauce
Dash of Tabasco sauce
$^{1}/_{4}$ cup finely chopped sweet pickle
$^{1}/_{4}$ cup finely chopped fresh Italian parsley
2 tablespoons finely chopped shallots
2 tablespoons small capers, finely chopped
Salt and pepper to taste

CRAB CAKES

1 pound lump crab meat
1 cup fine bread crumbs
6 tablespoons mayonnaise
2 tablespoons Dijon mustard
2 eggs, lightly beaten
2 tablespoons finely chopped fresh parsley
2 teaspoons Worcestershire sauce
4 green onions, finely chopped
Unsalted butter

For the sauce, combine the mayonnaise, lemon juice, Worcestershire sauce and Tabasco sauce in a bowl and mix well. Fold in the pickle, parsley, shallots, capers, salt and pepper. Chill, covered, for 1 to 8 hours.

For the crab cakes, combine the crab meat and bread crumbs in a bowl and mix lightly.

Combine the next six ingredients in a bowl and mix well. Fold in the crab meat mixture gently. Shape into patties and place on a plate. Chill, covered, for up to 8 hours. Melt the butter in a skillet. Add the crab cakes and cook for 3 to 4 minutes per side or until golden brown. Serve with the Tartar Sauce. *Serves 4.*

GRILLED HALIBUT

2 garlic cloves, crushed
$^{1}/_{4}$ teaspoon white pepper
2 tablespoons sugar
$^{1}/_{3}$ cup soy sauce

6 tablespoons corn oil
3 green onions, chopped
1 tablespoon sesame seeds
2 (1-inch-thick) halibut steaks

Combine the garlic, white pepper, sugar, soy sauce, corn oil, green onions and sesame seeds in a bowl and mix well. Pour over the halibut steaks in a shallow dish.

Chill, covered, overnight. Remove the fish and discard the marinade. Grill the halibut steaks for 7 minutes per side or until the fish flakes easily. *Serves 2.*

ROASTED HALIBUT WITH FRESH HERB SAUCE

FRESH HERB SAUCE
$^1/_2$ cup extra-virgin olive oil
$^1/_4$ cup finely chopped fresh flat-leaf parsley
$^1/_4$ cup finely chopped arugula
1 tablespoon finely chopped fresh marjoram
1 tablespoon finely chopped fresh oregano
1 teaspoon minced garlic
2 teaspoons red wine vinegar
Kosher salt and pepper to taste

HALIBUT
1 cup coarsely ground fresh bread crumbs
1 tablespoon extra-virgin olive oil
1 teaspoon minced garlic
1 tablespoon dry white wine
6 (6-ounce) skinless halibut fillets
Kosher salt and pepper to taste

For the sauce, combine the olive oil, parsley, arugula, marjoram, oregano, garlic, vinegar, salt and pepper in a bowl and mix well.

For the halibut, combine the bread crumbs, olive oil, garlic and wine in a bowl and toss to coat. Spread over the bottom of a pie plate. Bake at 400 degrees for 8 minutes.

Arrange the fillets in a lightly oiled baking dish and season with salt and pepper. Bake at 400 degrees for 8 minutes. Top with the bread crumb mixture. Bake for 8 minutes longer or until the fish flakes easily. Remove to a serving platter and drizzle with the Fresh Herb Sauce. *Serves 6.*

Chardonnay is a tricky grape. It changes and adapts its flavor to meet all growing regions and styles. Chablis is the northernmost outpost for Chardonnay in Burgundy. Crisp, clean, bright, and refreshing, Chablis is the wine for mild yet richly textured seafood. Chablis pairs well with Grilled Halibut (page 104) and Roasted Halibut with Fresh Herb Sauce (above).

GARLICKY SCALLOPS AND SHRIMP

6 large sea scallops, rinsed, patted dry and halved
6 to 8 large peeled shrimp
Salt and freshly ground pepper to taste
All-purpose flour

2 to 3 tablespoons olive oil
1 garlic clove, minced
1 tablespoon chopped fresh basil
2 to 3 tablespoons fresh lemon juice

Season the scallops and shrimp with salt and pepper. Coat with the flour, shaking off any excess. Heat the olive oil in a large skillet over high heat. Add the scallops and shrimp and reduce the heat. Cook for 2 minutes. Turn over the scallops and shrimp and add the garlic and basil.

Shake the skillet to evenly distribute the scallops, shrimp, garlic and basil. Cook for 2 minutes or until the scallops and shrimp are golden brown and firm to the touch. Sprinkle with the lemon juice and toss to mix. *Serves 2 to 4.*

LINGUINI WITH SHRIMP AND SUN-DRIED TOMATOES

2 tablespoons butter
2 tablespoons olive oil
1 onion, chopped
4 garlic cloves, minced
1/2 cup oil-pack sun-dried tomatoes, drained and cut into strips
2 tablespoons capers, drained and rinsed
1/4 cup chopped fresh parsley

1/2 cup dry white wine
24 large peeled shrimp
1/2 cup half-and-half
2 tablespoons Dijon mustard
1/2 teaspoon salt
1/2 teaspoon freshly ground pepper
16 ounces linguini, cooked al dente and drained

Heat the butter and olive oil in a skillet. Add the onion and garlic and sauté until tender. Stir in the sun-dried tomatoes, capers and parsley. Stir in the wine. Simmer for 2 minutes. Stir in the shrimp.

Simmer for 2 minutes or until the shrimp turn pink. Stir in the half-and-half and Dijon mustard. Cook until heated through. Stir in the salt and pepper. Serve over the hot linguini. *Serves 4.*

SEAFOOD STEW WITH TOMATOES, SHRIMP AND SCALLOPS

1/4 cup olive oil

2 yellow onions, chopped (about 1 1/2 cups)

4 small carrots, cut into 1/4-inch pieces (about 1 cup)

1 teaspoon chopped garlic

2 (28-ounce) cans plum tomatoes, drained and cut into 1/2-inch pieces

4 cups chicken broth

2/3 cup dry white wine

2 tablespoons chopped fresh basil

2 teaspoons grated orange zest

1/2 teaspoon red pepper flakes

1/2 teaspoon salt

1 pound Chilean sea bass, halibut or other firm white fish fillets, cut into 1 1/2-inch pieces

12 ounces sea scallops

12 ounces large deveined peeled shrimp

2 tablespoons julienned fresh basil leaves

6 (1/2-inch-thick) orange wedges

Heat the olive oil in a heavy saucepan over medium heat. Add the onions and carrots and sauté for 4 minutes or until tender-crisp. Add the garlic and sauté for 1 minute. Stir in the tomatoes, broth, wine, chopped basil, orange zest, red pepper flakes and salt. Bring to a simmer and reduce the heat to low. Cook for 10 minutes, stirring occasionally. Stir in the fish. Simmer for 3 minutes.

Stir in the scallops and shrimp. Simmer for 2 to 3 minutes or until the scallops are tender and the shrimp turn pink. Adjust the seasonings. Ladle equal portions into six shallow serving bowls and sprinkle each with 1 teaspoon of the julienned basil leaves. Place one orange wedge on the edge of each bowl. Squeeze the orange juice into the stew before eating. *Serves 6.*

Parsley Purée

Combine 1 bunch of parsley, 1 tablespoon capers, 1/2 small red onion, juice of 1 lemon, 3/4 cup olive oil, and salt and pepper to taste in a blender and blend until smooth. Serve with fish.

COD WITH TOMATO AND ARTICHOKE SAUCE

2 (6-ounce) jars marinated artichoke hearts
1 teaspoon minced garlic
1/2 cup chopped onion
1/2 cup thinly sliced celery
1/4 cup tomato paste
1 (28-ounce) can tomatoes, chopped
1/2 cup dry white wine

1/2 teaspoon oregano
1/2 teaspoon basil
1/2 teaspoon salt
1/2 teaspoon freshly ground pepper
12 ounces cod or orange roughy fillets
1 tablespoon finely chopped fresh parsley

Drain the artichoke hearts, reserving 3 tablespoons of the marinade. Combine the reserved marinade, garlic and onion in a large skillet. Sauté over medium heat for 2 minutes or until tender. Stir in the celery. Stir in the tomato paste, tomatoes, wine, oregano, basil, salt and pepper. Bring to a boil over medium heat.

Cook for 10 to 15 minutes or until slightly thickened. Stir in the artichoke hearts. Place the fillets gently on top. Cook for 20 minutes or until the fish flakes easily, basting gently with the sauce once or twice. Remove the fillets with a spatula to serving plates. Spoon the sauce over the fillets and sprinkle with the parsley. *Serves 4.*

ORIENTAL GROUPER

1/4 cup orange juice
1/4 cup soy sauce
2 tablespoons ketchup
2 tablespoons butter, melted
2 tablespoons chopped fresh parsley
1 tablespoon lemon juice

1 garlic clove, minced
1/2 teaspoon oregano
1/2 teaspoon pepper
Salt to taste
2 pounds grouper fillets

Combine the orange juice, soy sauce, ketchup, melted butter, parsley, lemon juice, garlic, oregano, pepper and salt in a bowl and mix well.

Pour over the fillets in a shallow dish. Chill, covered, for 1 hour. Remove the fillets and discard the marinade. Broil or grill the fillets until the fish flakes easily. *Serves 4.*

ONE-DISH SALMON

1 tablespoon olive oil
2 leeks, rinsed and cut into large slices
8 to 10 small red potatoes
6 carrots, cut diagonally into large slices
2/3 cup dry white wine
1 bunch Swiss chard, kale or spinach,
stems removed and leaves roughly torn
2 pounds skinless salmon fillets,
cut into serving-size pieces
1/4 cup (1/2 stick) butter, cut into pieces
2 tablespoons Dijon mustard

Heat the olive oil in a large heavy saucepan over medium heat. Add the leeks and sauté for 3 minutes or just until wilted. Stir in the potatoes, carrots and wine. Cook, covered, for 15 minutes. Add the Swiss chard and cook, covered, for 5 minutes. Arrange the fillets in a single layer on top of the Swiss chard.

Dot the fillets with the butter. Cook, covered, for 10 to 15 minutes or just until the fish flakes easily. Remove the fillets and vegetables carefully to a warm serving platter. Whisk the Dijon mustard into the saucepan. Pour the sauce evenly over the fillets on the platter and serve immediately. *Serves 4.*

While cooking fish or vegetables that give off unpleasant odors, simmer a small pan of vinegar on top of the stove.

CHILLED POACHED SALMON WITH MUSTARD DILL SAUCE

1 bunch fresh dill weed sprigs
2 to 3 pounds fresh salmon, rinsed and patted dry
1 cup dry white wine
1 tablespoon fresh lemon juice

1 teaspoon salt
1/2 cup sour cream
1/4 cup Dijon mustard
1/4 cup mayonnaise
Chopped fresh dill weed to taste

Line a 9×13-inch glass baking dish with the dill weed sprigs. Place the salmon on top of the dill weed. Pour the wine and lemon juice over the top and sprinkle with the salt. Cover tightly with foil. Bake at 400 degrees for 25 minutes or until the fish flakes easily. Remove the salmon from the liquid and let cool slightly.

Skin the salmon and place on a serving platter. Cover and chill thoroughly. Combine the sour cream, Dijon mustard, mayonnaise and chopped dill weed in a bowl and mix well. Cover and chill thoroughly. Serve the chilled sauce with the chilled salmon. *Serves 6 to 8.*

SEARED ROASTED SALMON FILLETS WITH LEMON GINGER BUTTER

6 tablespoons butter, softened
2 tablespoons fresh lemon juice, slightly warmed
2 tablespoons minced fresh ginger
2 tablespoons finely chopped fresh chives
4 (5-ounce) salmon fillets, skinned and patted dry
Kosher salt and freshly ground pepper to taste
Olive oil

Combine the butter, lemon juice, ginger and chives in a bowl and mix well. Season the fillets lightly with salt and pepper. Coat an ovenproof skillet lightly with olive oil. Heat over medium-high heat until hot. Add the fillets skinned side up.

Cook the fillets for 1 minute or until golden brown. Turn over the fillets. Bake at 500 degrees for 2 minutes for medium-rare to 4 minutes for medium-well. Remove the fillets to serving plates and top each fillet with a dollop of the lemon ginger butter. *Serves 4.*

SPECIAL GRILLED SALMON

2 pounds salmon fillets
1/4 cup Triple Sec or Cointreau
2 tablespoons brown sugar
1 tablespoon lime juice
1 teaspoon pressed garlic

Place the fillets skin side down on a large sheet of heavy-duty foil sprayed with nonstick cooking spray. Combine the liqueur, brown sugar, lime juice and garlic in a bowl and mix well. Pour over the fillets and baste several times to coat. Seal the foil around the fillets. Chill, covered, for at least 1 hour.

Place the foil packet over hot coals and grill for 5 to 6 minutes or until the fish flakes easily. Remove the foil packet to a heatproof work surface and open carefully. Slide a spatula between the fillets and the foil to release the fillets and leave the skin on the foil. Remove the fillets to serving plates. *Serves 4.*

California Pinot Noir from Santa Barbara is married to grilled or pan-seared salmon. They seem to be made for each other. The crusty charred flavor that salmon gets from the pan or grill rolls into the sharp but creamy fruit of Pinot Noir from Santa Barbara. Sanford and Fess Parker are safe bets for the table. California Pinot Noir pairs especially well with Special Grilled Salmon (above) and Seared Roasted Salmon Fillets with Lemon Ginger Butter (page 110).

SPICED SALMON WITH YELLOW PEPPERS

$1/2$ teaspoon salt
1 teaspoon minced garlic
1 teaspoon oregano
1 teaspoon paprika
$1/2$ teaspoon cumin
Freshly ground pepper
1 teaspoon olive oil
1 (12-ounce) salmon fillet, patted dry and cut into 2 pieces
2 teaspoons olive oil
1 small yellow bell pepper, seeded and cut into $1/4$-inch strips
$1^1/2$ teaspoons olive oil
$1/4$ cup fresh orange juice

Combine the salt, garlic, oregano, paprika, cumin and a few grinds of pepper in a bowl and mix well. Remove $1/2$ heaping teaspoon and set aside. Add 1 teaspoon olive oil to the remaining spice mixture and stir to form a paste. Rub evenly over the nonskin side of the fillets. Heat 2 teaspoons olive oil in a nonstick skillet over medium heat. Add the bell pepper and sauté for 8 to 10 minutes or until tender and beginning to brown. Remove the bell pepper to a bowl.

Add $1^1/2$ teaspoons olive oil to the skillet. Heat over medium-high heat until hot. Add the fillets skin side up and cook for 3 to 4 minutes. Turn over the fillets. Cook, covered, for 4 to 5 minutes for medium. Remove the fillets to serving plates and keep warm. Add the bell pepper, orange juice and reserved spice mix to the skillet. Cook over high heat for 3 to 4 minutes or until syrupy, stirring occasionally. Spoon over the fillets and serve. *Serves 2.*

HOISIN-GLAZED SEA BASS

2 tablespoons hoisin sauce
1 tablespoon soy sauce
1 teaspoon toasted sesame oil

$1/4$ teaspoon pepper
4 (4- to 6-ounce) sea bass fillets
  (about 1 inch thick)

Combine the hoisin sauce, soy sauce, sesame oil and pepper in a bowl and mix well. Pat the fillets dry.

Brush the sauce evenly over the fillets. Grill or broil for 5 minutes per side or until the fish flakes easily. *Serves 4.*

HONEY SOY AHI TUNA STEAKS

$1/4$ cup soy sauce
2 tablespoons honey
1 tablespoon toasted sesame oil

1 tablespoon grated fresh ginger
$1/2$ teaspoon freshly ground pepper
4 ahi tuna steaks

Combine the soy sauce, honey, sesame oil, ginger and pepper in a bowl and mix well. Pour over the tuna steaks in a shallow dish and turn to coat.

Marinate for 30 minutes. Remove the tuna steaks and discard the marinade. Grill for 2 to 3 minutes per side. *Serves 4.*

Remember the old days when the rule was "no red wine with fish"? Well, those days are gone. Red Zinfandel can do wonders with grilled fish, especially a Zinfandel with an Asian flair. Avoid any Zinfandel that has an alcohol level higher than 15 percent (they are too heavy). Cline, Rosenblum, and Rancho Zabacco are great lightweight Zinfandels. Try them with Hoisin-Glazed Sea Bass (above), Honey Soy Ahi Tuna Steaks (above), or Oriental Grouper (page 108).

BOW TIE PASTA WITH FRESH TOMATO BASIL SAUCE

4 large vine-ripened tomatoes,
peeled and chopped (about 4 cups)
2 garlic cloves, minced
3 tablespoons chopped fresh basil
3 tablespoons extra-virgin olive oil
1 tablespoon balsamic vinegar
$1/2$ teaspoon salt
$1/2$ teaspoon freshly ground pepper
6 ounces bowtie pasta, cooked and drained
1 (4-ounce) package crumbled goat cheese

Combine the tomatoes, garlic, basil, olive oil, vinegar, salt and pepper in a bowl and mix well. Let stand for 1 hour at room temperature.

Spoon the tomato mixture over the hot pasta on serving plates and sprinkle with the cheese. Garnish with fresh basil sprigs, if desired. *Serves 2 or 3.*

DRY RUB FOR BEEF, PORK OR POULTRY BARBECUE

$1/2$ cup sugar
2 tablespoons seasoned salt
2 tablespoons garlic salt
2 tablespoons onion salt
2 tablespoons paprika
2 tablespoons chili powder
2 tablespoons pepper
2 teaspoons celery seeds
2 teaspoons oregano

$1/2$ teaspoon cumin
$1/2$ teaspoon nutmeg
$1/2$ teaspoon ground cinnamon
$1/2$ teaspoon fennel seeds
$1/2$ teaspoon dry mustard
6 whole cloves, or
   $1/2$ teaspoon ground cloves
1 small bay leaf

Combine the sugar, seasoned salt, garlic salt, onion salt, paprika, chili powder, pepper, celery seeds, oregano, cumin, nutmeg, cinnamon, fennel seeds, dry mustard, cloves and bay leaf in a food processor and process to a powder. Rub spare ribs, beef brisket, beef eye-of-round or chicken pieces generously with the dry rub.

Chill, covered, for 1 to 2 days. Grill over indirect low heat for up to 3 hours. Baste with your favorite barbecue sauce during the last 30 minutes of grilling, watching carefully so that the sauce doesn't burn. Store the dry rub in an airtight container in a cool dry place or in the refrigerator. *Makes 3/4 cup.*

Blue Cheese Polenta 119

Spinach Feta Rice 119

Creamy Lemon Rice 120

Artichoke and Spinach Casserole 120

Marinated Green Beans
   with Red Onion 121

Northern Bean Casserole 121

Brussels Sprouts in Pecan Butter 122

Sweet-and-Sour Red Cabbage
   with Apples 122

Cauliflower Purée in Tomato Cups 123

Mashed Cauliflower 123

Corn Casserole 124

Easy Ratatouille 124

Crispy Eggplant 125

Stuffed Mushrooms 125

Onions with Currant, Port
   and Balsamic Glaze 126

Spicy Pimentos 126

Scalloped Potatoes 127

Oven Potato Puff 128

Roasted Curried Sweet Potatoes 128

Butternut Squash with a Twist 129

Tomato Chutney 129

Zucchini and Summer
   Squash Gratin 130

Cold Vegetables
   with Mustard Sauce 131

Cranberry Conserve 132

Cantaloupe and Cherry Tomato Salsa . . 132

Pineapple Avocado Salsa 133

Baked Pineapple 133

SIDE DISHES

Side Dishes

The setting on the facing page was designed and the accessories were selected by Martha Quay and Jane James of Veranda, Bloomfield Hills, Michigan, and photographed by Martha Quay in The Village Club living room.

6

SIDE DISHES

Side Dishes

MURAL IN THE LIVING ROOM CIRCA 1961

Above a small balcony in the living room of the Winningham House was found one of several murals, which depicted scenes from the story of Robin Hood and his band of merry men. Charles Winningham's knowledge and fondness of Robin Hood lore gave the house the nickname of Robin Hood's Barn. When renovating, The Village Club donated the murals to a children's hospital.

BLUE CHEESE POLENTA

1 small onion, chopped (optional)
6 tablespoons unsalted butter
2 cups milk
3/4 cup cornmeal
5 ounces blue cheese, crumbled
1 teaspoon nutmeg
2 to 3 teaspoons kosher salt
1/2 cup heavy cream
Pepper to taste

Sauté the onion in the butter in a saucepan until tender. Stir in the milk. Bring to a boil. Stir in the cornmeal gradually. Cook until thick enough to hold a spoon upright, stirring constantly. Add the cheese, nutmeg and salt. Cook until the cheese is melted, stirring constantly.

Remove from the heat and beat in the cream and pepper. Spoon into buttered muffin cups and let cool until set. Remove the polenta muffins to a baking pan. Sprinkle the tops with additional blue cheese, if desired. Bake at 400 degrees for 15 minutes. *Serves 6.*

SPINACH FETA RICE

1 cup basmati rice
2 1/4 cups chicken broth
1 onion, chopped
1 cup sliced mushrooms
2 garlic cloves, minced
Vegetable oil

1 tablespoon lemon juice
1/2 teaspoon oregano
6 cups shredded fresh spinach
4 ounces feta cheese, crumbled
Pepper to taste

Combine the rice and broth in a saucepan. Bring to a boil and stir. Reduce the heat and cook, covered, for 35 to 45 minutes or until the liquid is absorbed. Sauté the onion, mushrooms and garlic in a small amount of oil in a skillet until the vegetables are tender.

Add the lemon juice and oregano to the onion mixture and mix well. Add to the rice. Stir in the spinach, cheese and pepper. Cook until the spinach is wilted, tossing constantly. *Serves 4.*

CREAMY LEMON RICE

1/2 cup (1 stick) unsalted butter
2 cups long grain white rice
Grated zest of 2 lemons
3 cups boiling chicken broth

1 teaspoon salt
2 tablespoons fresh lemon juice
1 cup heavy cream
Freshly ground white pepper to taste

Melt the butter in a saucepan over low heat. Stir in the rice and lemon zest. Cook over medium heat for 5 minutes or until the rice is opaque, stirring constantly. Stir in the broth and salt. Simmer, covered, for 20 minutes or until the liquid is absorbed.

Stir in the lemon juice. Stir in the cream gradually. Cook over low heat until the cream is absorbed. Season with white pepper. Garnish with lemon zest strips and chopped fresh parsley. *Serves 8 to 10.*

ARTICHOKE AND SPINACH CASSEROLE

1 (14-ounce) can artichoke hearts, drained
1/2 (8-ounce) can sliced water chestnuts, drained
2 (10-ounce) packages frozen chopped spinach, thawed, drained and squeezed dry
8 ounces cream cheese, softened

1/2 cup (1 stick) butter, melted
2 teaspoons Worcestershire sauce
1/2 teaspoon garlic salt
Bread crumbs
Grated Romano cheese

Cut the artichokes into quarters. Combine the water chestnuts and spinach in a bowl and mix well. Spoon into a baking dish sprayed with nonstick cooking spray.

Beat the cream cheese, melted butter, Worcestershire sauce and garlic salt in a bowl. Pour over the artichoke mixture. Sprinkle with bread crumbs and Romano cheese. Bake at 350 degrees for 30 minutes. *Serves 6.*

When removing the zest from an orange, lemon, or lime, be careful to avoid the spongy, white, bitter-tasting pith just beneath the skin. A zester will remove the zest only. Remember, zest dries out quickly—don't remove it until you're ready to use it.

MARINATED GREEN BEANS WITH RED ONION

Salt to taste
1 pound green beans, trimmed
1/2 small red onion, cut into thin slivers (about 1/2 cup)
2 or 3 garlic cloves, crushed
1/2 cup olive oil
1/4 teaspoon salt
Freshly ground pepper
3 tablespoons chopped fresh dill weed
3 to 4 tablespoons fresh lemon juice

Bring a large saucepan of lightly salted water to a boil. Add the beans gradually. Cook for 3 to 4 minutes or just until tender-crisp. Drain in a colander. Plunge into ice water until cool. Drain well and place in a bowl.

Add the onion, garlic, olive oil, 1/4 teaspoon salt, pepper and dill weed. Toss gently to coat. Remove the garlic cloves and add the lemon juice. Toss to mix. Adjust the seasonings. Serve at room temperature. *Serves 4.*

NORTHERN BEAN CASSEROLE

4 slices bacon
2 onions, chopped
1 (48-ounce) jar Great Northern beans
1/2 cup sugar
1 tablespoon basil
1 teaspoon thyme
1 teaspoon seasoned salt

Cook the bacon in a saucepan until crisp. Remove to paper towels to drain; crumble. Add the onions to the bacon drippings and sauté until tender.

Stir in the beans, sugar, basil, thyme, seasoned salt and crumbled bacon. Spoon into a baking dish. Bake, covered, at 300 degrees for 2 hours. *Serves 8 to 10.*

BRUSSELS SPROUTS IN PECAN BUTTER

1 pound brussels sprouts, trimmed
Salt to taste
3 tablespoons unsalted butter
1/4 cup coarsely chopped pecans
Freshly ground pepper

Cut an X in the stem end of each brussels sprout. Cook the brussels sprouts, covered, in a saucepan of boiling salted water for 10 minutes or until tender; drain. Spread in a shallow serving dish and keep warm.

Cook the butter in a saucepan until it begins to brown. Add the pecans. Cook until the pecans are light brown; do not let burn. Pour the pecans and butter over the brussels sprouts and sprinkle with pepper. *Serves 4.*

SWEET-AND-SOUR RED CABBAGE WITH APPLES

1/4 cup (1/2 stick) butter
2 tablespoons sugar
1 onion, chopped
2 pounds red cabbage, finely shredded
2 tart apples, peeled, cored and thinly sliced
2 tablespoons cider vinegar
1/2 cup dry red wine
1/8 teaspoon cayenne pepper
1/2 cup water
Salt and freshly ground black pepper to taste

Melt the butter in a large saucepan over medium heat. Add the sugar and cook for 2 minutes, stirring constantly. Reduce the heat and add the onion. Cook until light brown, stirring occasionally. Stir in the cabbage, apples, vinegar, wine and cayenne pepper.

Cook the cabbage mixture, covered, over low heat for 10 minutes. Stir in the water. Cook, partially covered, for 30 to 40 minutes or until the liquid is absorbed, stirring occasionally. Season with salt and black pepper. *Serves 8.*

CAULIFLOWER PUREE IN TOMATO CUPS

4 cups cauliflower florets, steamed until tender
1 tablespoon butter
4^1/$_2$ teaspoons milk
Pinch of nutmeg
Salt and pepper to taste

4 tomatoes, halved crosswise
2 tablespoons butter
1 tablespoon Dijon mustard
1^1/$_2$ cups fresh bread crumbs
2 tablespoons chopped fresh parsley

Purée the cauliflower, 1 tablespoon butter, the milk, nutmeg, salt and pepper in a food processor. Scoop out the tomato halves, leaving a 1/2-inch shell; discard the pulp. Drain cut side down on paper towels. Arrange the tomatoes cut side up on a small baking sheet. Fill with the puréed cauliflower.

Melt 2 tablespoons butter in a skillet over medium heat. Stir in the Dijon mustard. Add the bread crumbs. Cook for 8 minutes or until beginning to brown, tossing constantly. Sprinkle over the filled tomatoes. Bake at 350 degrees for 30 minutes or until heated through. Sprinkle with the parsley. *Serves 8.*

MASHED CAULIFLOWER

1 head cauliflower
1 tablespoon (or more) butter

2 tablespoons (or more) half-and-half
Salt and pepper to taste

Cut the cauliflower into florets. Cook the florets in a saucepan of boiling water just until tender; drain well. Purée the cauliflower in a food processor or mash in a bowl with a potato masher. Add the butter, half-and-half, salt and pepper and process or mash until smooth. *Serves 4.*

Note: This recipe looks like, and can be substituted for, mashed potatoes.

*A*dd a little milk to cauliflower when cooking
and it will remain white.

CORN CASSEROLE

1/2 cup (1 stick) butter or margarine, melted
1 cup sour cream
1 egg

1 (8-ounce) package corn bread mix
1 (14-ounce) can whole kernel corn, drained
1 (14-ounce) can cream-style corn

Combine the melted butter and sour cream in a large bowl and mix well. Beat in the egg. Stir in the corn bread mix. Add the whole kernel corn and cream-style corn and mix well.

Pour into a 1³/4- to 2-quart baking dish sprayed with nonstick cooking spray. Bake at 350 degrees for 45 minutes or until the top is golden brown and a knife inserted in the center comes out clean. *Serves 6 to 8.*

EASY RATATOUILLE

3 tablespoons olive oil
1 cup chopped peeled eggplant
(1/2-inch pieces)
1/2 cup chopped onion
1/2 cup chopped yellow squash (1/2-inch pieces)
1/2 cup chopped zucchini (1/2-inch pieces)

1/2 cup chopped seeded peeled Italian plum
   tomatoes (about 2)
1/4 cup chopped fresh basil
2 tablespoons minced garlic
1 teaspoon salt
Freshly ground pepper to taste

Heat the olive oil in a large skillet over high heat. Add the eggplant, onion, yellow squash, zucchini, tomatoes, basil, garlic, salt and pepper.

Stir-fry the mixture for 5 to 8 minutes or until the vegetables are tender-crisp. Remove from the heat and serve. *Serves 4.*

*G*arlic is a member of the lily family. It grows underground as a bulb. Each bulb has twelve to twenty-four cloves that are held together by an outer skin. When purchasing garlic, look for a bulb that is firm without any brown spots or sprouts.

CRISPY EGGPLANT

$^1/_3$ cup bread crumbs
$^1/_3$ cup grated Parmesan cheese
1 teaspoon Italian herb seasoning
$^1/_3$ cup mayonnaise
2 tablespoons dried onion flakes
1 eggplant, peeled and cut into $^1/_2$-inch slices

Combine the bread crumbs, cheese and herb seasoning in a bowl and mix well. Spread half the bread crumb mixture over the bottom of a baking pan. Combine the mayonnaise and onion flakes in a bowl and mix well.

Spread the mayonnaise mixture over both sides of the eggplant slices. Arrange the eggplant in the baking pan and top with the remaining bread crumb mixture. Bake at 425 degrees for 20 to 30 minutes. *Serves 6.*

STUFFED MUSHROOMS

1 pound very large white mushrooms
$5^1/_3$ tablespoons butter
1 onion, finely chopped
$2^1/_4$ cups coarsely torn fresh bread crumbs
(from day-old bread)
$1^1/_2$ teaspoons salt

$^1/_4$ teaspoon pepper
2 tablespoons lemon juice
1 tablespoon ketchup
Bacon slices, cut into short thin strips
$^1/_2$ cup half-and-half

Clean the mushrooms and remove the stems. Chop the stems finely. Melt the butter in a skillet. Add the chopped mushroom stems and onion and sauté until the vegetables are tender. Add the bread crumbs and cook for 3 minutes, stirring frequently. Stir in the salt, pepper, lemon juice and ketchup.

Fill the mushroom caps with the bread crumb mixture. Arrange 2 strips of bacon in a cross pattern over each stuffed mushroom. Arrange the mushrooms in a baking dish. Pour the half-and-half around the mushrooms.

Bake at 400 degrees for 20 minutes. Garnish with chopped fresh parsley and serve with beef. *Serves 6.*

ONIONS WITH CURRANT, PORT AND BALSAMIC GLAZE

2 pounds small boiling onions
(³/4- to 1-inch diameter)
Salt to taste
1 cup (or more) ruby port
²/3 cup dried currants
3 tablespoons butter

2 tablespoons light brown sugar
1 tablespoon balsamic vinegar
2 teaspoons finely chopped fresh thyme
1 tablespoon balsamic vinegar
Pepper to taste
1 teaspoon finely chopped fresh thyme

Cook the onions in a saucepan of boiling salted water for 2 minutes. Drain and let cool slightly. Peel the onions and cut off the root end. Combine the onions, port, currants, butter, brown sugar, 1 tablespoon vinegar and 2 teaspoons thyme in a heavy skillet and cover.

Bring to a boil. Reduce the heat to medium. Cook, covered, for 15 minutes. Cook, uncovered, for 10 minutes or until the onions are tender-crisp and coated with the glaze, stirring frequently. Stir in 1 tablespoon vinegar, salt and pepper. Sprinkle with 1 teaspoon thyme. *Serves 6.*

SPICY PIMENTOS

4 red bell peppers
2 to 3 tablespoons chicken broth or water
2 tablespoons olive oil
4 garlic cloves, crushed slightly
¹/4 teaspoon cayenne pepper
Salt to taste

Place the bell peppers in a roasting pan. Roast at 375 degrees for 17 minutes. Turn over the bell peppers and roast for 17 minutes longer. Cover the pan tightly with foil and let cool. Remove the bell peppers and stir the broth into the roasting pan, scraping any brown bits from the bottom of the pan.

Peel, seed and slice each bell pepper into eight strips. Heat the olive oil in a heavy skillet over low heat until warm but not sizzling. Add the bell peppers, garlic, cayenne pepper and salt. Cook for 3 minutes, stirring frequently. Stir in the roasting pan juices. Cook, covered, for 5 minutes. Cool to room temperature; serve. *Serves 4.*

SCALLOPED POTATOES

4 ounces extra-sharp Cheddar cheese, shredded
4 ounces Danish blue cheese, crumbled
$1/3$ cup (about) freshly grated Parmesan cheese
4 pounds russet potatoes, peeled and cut into $1/4$-inch slices
$1^{1/2}$ teaspoons salt
$1/2$ teaspoon pepper
$1/4$ cup finely chopped onion
3 tablespoons all-purpose flour
$1/4$ cup ($1/2$ stick) butter
3 cups hot milk

Combine the Cheddar cheese, blue cheese and Parmesan cheese in a bowl and mix well. Arrange half the potatoes in a lightly buttered 9×13-inch baking dish, slightly overlapping the slices. Sprinkle with half the salt and half the pepper. Sprinkle with the onion. Sprinkle with the flour and dot with half the butter. Sprinkle with half the cheese mixture.

Top with the remaining potatoes, salt, pepper and butter. Pour the hot milk evenly over the top. Cover tightly with foil. Bake at 400 degrees for 45 minutes. Remove the foil and sprinkle the potatoes with the remaining cheese mixture. Bake, uncovered, for 45 minutes or until the potatoes are tender and the cheese is golden brown. Let stand for 15 minutes before serving. *Serves 12.*

*P*otatoes will stay fresh and firm longer if you store them in a bag along with an apple. The apple gives off a gas that prevents potatoes from sprouting.

OVEN POTATO PUFF

1 cup small curd cottage cheese
2 eggs
1 cup sour cream
1/3 cup chopped green onions
1/4 cup (1/2 stick) butter, softened

1 teaspoon salt
1/8 teaspoon pepper
6 large white potatoes, peeled, quartered, cooked
   and mashed (about 6 cups)
2 tablespoons butter, melted

Combine the cottage cheese and eggs in a bowl. Beat with an electric mixer at high speed for 2 minutes or until almost smooth. Beat in the sour cream, green onions, 1/4 cup butter, the salt and pepper at low speed.

Beat in the mashed potatoes. Spoon into a buttered 2-quart baking dish. Drizzle with 2 tablespoons melted butter. Bake at 325 degrees for 50 minutes or until heated through and light brown on top. *Serves 8 to 10.*

ROASTED CURRIED SWEET POTATOES

1 1/2 tablespoons unsalted butter
1/2 teaspoon curry powder
Salt and pepper to taste
12 ounces sweet potatoes, peeled and
cut into 1-inch pieces (about 2 cups)

Melt the butter in a small saucepan. Stir in the curry powder, salt and pepper. Combine the curry mixture and sweet potatoes in a small baking pan and toss to coat.

Bake at 450 degrees for 15 to 20 minutes or until the sweet potatoes are tender and golden brown, shaking the pan occasionally to mix. *Serves 2.*

If you have peeled too many potatoes for your recipe, cover them with cold water to which a few drops of vinegar have been added. If kept refrigerated, they will last for three to four days.

BUTTERNUT SQUASH WITH A TWIST

1 (2¹/₄-pound) butternut squash, peeled, seeded and
cut into 1¹/₂-inch pieces
1¹/₂ cups seedless red grapes (about 8 ounces)
1 onion, cut into 1-inch pieces
1 tablespoon thinly sliced fresh sage leaves
2 tablespoons extra-virgin olive oil
2 tablespoons unsalted butter, melted
Salt and pepper to taste
¹/₄ cup pine nuts, toasted

Combine the squash, grapes, onion and sage in a bowl. Drizzle with the olive oil and melted butter. Season generously with salt and pepper and toss well to coat. Spread over the bottom of a 10×15-inch baking pan.

Bake at 425 degrees for 50 minutes or until the squash and onion are beginning to brown, stirring occasionally. Remove to a serving platter and sprinkle with the pine nuts. *Serves 4 to 6.*

TOMATO CHUTNEY

3 cups finely chopped peeled tomatoes (about 4)
1 cup finely chopped red bell pepper
1 cup finely chopped red onion
¹/₂ cup sweetened dried cranberries
¹/₂ cup cider vinegar
¹/₄ cup granulated sugar
¹/₄ cup packed brown sugar

2 tablespoons minced fresh ginger
¹/₂ teaspoon salt
¹/₂ teaspoon mustard seeds
¹/₄ teaspoon ground cinnamon
¹/₄ teaspoon cumin
¹/₄ teaspoon ground allspice
¹/₈ teaspoon cayenne pepper

Combine the tomatoes, bell pepper, onion, dried cranberries, vinegar, granulated sugar, brown sugar, ginger, salt, mustard seeds, cinnamon, cumin, allspice and cayenne pepper in a saucepan and mix well. Bring to a boil and reduce the heat. Simmer, uncovered, for 45 minutes or until thick, stirring frequently.

Remove from the heat and let cool. Pour into airtight containers and store in the refrigerator or freezer for up to 2 months. *Makes 3¹/₂ cups.*

Note: Serve over crackers, burgers, or grilled chicken. Mix with mayonnaise to make a dip for fresh vegetables.

ZUCCHINI AND SUMMER SQUASH GRATIN

2 onions, thinly sliced
2 tablespoons olive oil
1 tablespoon fresh thyme
12 ounces (about 2 small) zucchini,
    cut diagonally into $1/4$-inch slices
12 ounces (about 2 small) yellow summer squash,
    cut diagonally into $1/4$-inch slices
$41/2$ teaspoons olive oil
2 tablespoons fresh thyme

$1/2$ teaspoon kosher salt
$11/4$ cups (5 ounces) freshly grated
    Parmigiano-Reggiano cheese
1 tablespoon fresh thyme
$11/4$ pounds small ripe tomatoes, cored,
    cut into $1/4$-inch slices and drained
Freshly ground pepper to taste
$1/2$ teaspoon kosher salt
$41/2$ teaspoons olive oil

Sauté the onions in 2 tablespoons olive oil in a skillet over medium heat for 20 minutes or until tender and golden brown. Spread the onions over the bottom of an oiled 2-quart shallow oval baking dish and let cool. Sprinkle 1 tablespoon thyme over the onions. Combine the zucchini, yellow squash, $41/2$ teaspoons olive oil, 2 tablespoons thyme and $1/2$ teaspoon salt in a bowl and toss to coat. Mix half the cheese and 1 tablespoon thyme in a bowl. Place a row of slightly overlapping tomato slices over the onions across the width of the baking dish. Sprinkle with some of the plain cheese. Place a row of slightly overlapping zucchini slices across the width of the baking dish, overlapping the tomato slices by two-thirds.

Sprinkle with some of the plain cheese. Place a row of slightly overlapping yellow squash slices across the width of the baking dish, overlapping the zucchini slices by two-thirds. Sprinkle with some of the plain cheese. Repeat the rows until the baking dish is full and all the tomatoes, zucchini, yellow squash and plain cheese have been used.

Sprinkle with pepper and $1/2$ teaspoon salt. Drizzle with $41/2$ teaspoons olive oil. Sprinkle with the cheese and thyme mixture. Bake at 375 degrees for 65 to 70 minutes or until the top is golden brown and the juices have been reduced. Let stand for 15 minutes before serving. *Serves 6 to 8.*

COLD VEGETABLES WITH MUSTARD SAUCE

4 carrots, julienned
4 zucchini, seeded and julienned
4 yellow summer squash, seeded and julienned
1¹/2 pounds small green beans
1¹/2 pounds very small new red potatoes
1 tablespoon minced shallots
2 tablespoons Dijon mustard

3 tablespoons boiling water
¹/2 cup olive oil
Salt and freshly ground pepper to taste
Fresh lemon juice to taste
2 tablespoons finely chopped fresh parsley
   or other herb

Steam the carrots over a saucepan of boiling water just until tender-crisp. Rinse in cold water and remove to paper towels to drain. Place in a sealable plastic bag and chill until cold. Steam the zucchini over a saucepan of boiling water just until tender-crisp. Rinse in cold water and remove to paper towels to drain. Place in a sealable plastic bag and chill until cold. Steam the summer squash over a saucepan of boiling water just until tender-crisp. Rinse in cold water and remove to paper towels to drain. Place in a sealable plastic bag and chill until cold. Steam the beans over a saucepan of boiling water for 4 to 8 minutes or just until tender-crisp. Rinse in cold water and remove to paper towels to drain. Place in a sealable plastic bag and chill until cold.

Cook the potatoes in a saucepan of boiling water for 5 to 8 minutes or just until tender. Rinse in cold water and remove to paper towels to drain. Place in a sealable plastic bag and chill until cold. Combine the shallots and Dijon mustard in a warm bowl. Whisk in 3 tablespoons boiling water a few drops at a time. Whisk in the olive oil in a steady stream. Whisk in the salt, pepper, lemon juice and parsley.

Combine the carrots, zucchini and summer squash in a bowl. Add 3 tablespoons of the Dijon mustard sauce and toss lightly to coat. Arrange on a serving platter. Slice the potatoes thinly and arrange on the serving platter. Arrange the beans on the serving platter. Drizzle the remaining Dijon mustard sauce over the top. *Serves 8.*

*F*or a nice, caramelized crust on roasted vegetables, preheat a skillet in a hot oven for 15 minutes. Meanwhile, toss the vegetables with olive oil, salt and pepper. Add the vegetables to the preheated skillet. They'll sizzle when they hit the hot pan, creating a beautiful, caramelized crust.

CRANBERRY CONSERVE

1 thin-skinned orange, seeded and cut into pieces
1 pound (4 cups) fresh cranberries
1/2 cup dried currants
2 cups packed brown sugar

1 teaspoon ground cinnamon
1/2 teaspoon ground cloves
1/2 teaspoon salt
1 cup chopped walnuts

Chop the orange coarsely in a food processor. Combine the orange, cranberries, dried currants, brown sugar, cinnamon, cloves and salt in a heavy saucepan. Cook over medium heat for 10 to 12 minutes or until the cranberries pop, stirring frequently.

Remove from the heat and skim the foam. Stir in the walnuts. Pour into sterilized airtight containers and freeze. *Makes 4 cups.*

Note: Serve this with poultry or pork. It is also good served over Brie with crackers.

CANTALOUPE AND CHERRY TOMATO SALSA

2 cups chopped cantaloupe
2 cups halved cherry tomatoes
1/4 cup finely chopped shallots
1/4 cup chopped fresh oregano or basil
2 tablespoons finely chopped seeded jalapeño chile

2 tablespoons grated orange zest
2 tablespoons orange juice
2 tablespoons lime juice
1/4 teaspoon salt
1/8 teaspoon pepper

Combine the cantaloupe, tomatoes, shallots, oregano, jalapeño, orange zest, orange juice, lime juice, salt and pepper in a bowl and toss to coat.

Spoon the salsa into a serving dish. Chill, covered, for 30 minutes before serving. *Serves 6.*

PINEAPPLE AVOCADO SALSA

1 cup (1/4-inch pieces) fresh pineapple
2 plum tomatoes, seeded and
  cut into 1/4-inch pieces
1 avocado, cut into 1/4-inch pieces
1/2 cup chopped sweet onion
1/4 cup chopped fresh cilantro

1 1/2 teaspoons finely chopped jalapeño chile
  with seeds
3 tablespoons fresh lime juice
3 tablespoons fresh orange juice
3 tablespoons extra-virgin olive oil

Combine the pineapple, tomatoes, avocado, onion, cilantro, jalapeño, lime juice, orange juice and olive oil in a bowl and toss to coat.

Spoon the salsa into a serving dish. Chill, covered, until ready to serve. *Serves 6.*

BAKED PINEAPPLE

1/2 cup (1 stick) butter, softened
1 cup sugar
4 eggs, beaten

1 (16-ounce) can crushed pineapple, drained
5 slices white bread, crusts removed and
  bread cubed

Beat the butter and sugar in a bowl until light and fluffy. Beat in the eggs. Add the pineapple and mix well.

Fold in the bread cubes. Pour into a greased 1 1/2-quart baking dish. Bake at 350 degrees for 1 hour. *Serves 4.*

Cilantro, coriander, and Chinese parsley are the same herb (*Coriandum sativum*). Cilantro could possibly be the first spice used by mankind, as early as 5000 B.C. It is said to have been growing in the Hanging Gardens of Babylon, is mentioned in the Medical Papyrus of Thebes (1522 B.C.), and was placed in Egyptian tombs more than 3,000 years ago.

Double-Chocolate Mousse Cake.............137

Molten Chocolate Cakes.........................138

Apple and Nut Upside-Down Cake 138

Decadent Bread Pudding 139

Holiday Cranberry Steamed Pudding......139

Sticky Date Pudding
    with Caramel Sauce...........................140

Lemon Delicacy...................................141

Mousse in a Minute 141

White Forest Torte 142

Fabulous Raspberry Cheesecake 142

Hollywood's Favorite Cheesecake...........143

Easy Oreo Ice Cream 143

Frozen Lemon Cream 144

Ice Cream Pie Spectacular 144

Praline Ice Cream Pie
    with Caramel Sauce...........................145

Fig Compote with Honey and Thyme 145

Baked Manchego Cheese with
    Pear Compote and Sliced Pears...........146

Pears Poached in Spiced Red Wine..........147

Poached Pears with Cinnamon
    Ice Cream and Strawberry
    Raspberry Coulis...............................147

Rhubarb Squares...................................148

Strawberry Pavlova...............................148

Fruit Salsa Sundaes 149

Splendid Fruit Crisp 149

Black Russian Cake 150

Blueberry Pound Cake 150

Getty Museum Carrot Cake...................151

Ginger Cake in a Blackened Skillet 151

Luscious Lemon Cake............................152

Pumpkin Cake Roll 153

Pecan Date Pie 153

Summer Blueberry Raspberry Pie............154

Unhumble Raspberry Chocolate Pie 155

Tarte Tatin 156

Torta di Lemone 157

Butter Tart Squares 158

Good and Easy Brownies 158

Grasshopper Bars 159

Inventory Bars 160

Imperial Squares 160

Lemon Cornmeal Shortbread Bars..........161

Triple-Chocolate Biscotti 161

Pecan and Ginger Biscotti......................162

Chewy Chocolate Chip
    Oatmeal Cookies...............................163

Chocolate Truffle Cookies.....................163

Coconut Macaroons 164

Flourless Peanut Butter Cookies.............164

Forget 'em Meringues 165

Sesame Cookies 165

Almond Coconut Fudge
    Sundae Topping 166

Warm Blueberry Sauce..........................166

Salted Creamy Caramel Sauce.................167

A Pitcher of Hummers...........................167

Mocha Coffee 168

DESSERTS

Desserts

The setting on the facing page was designed and the accessories were selected by Dulce Fuller of Woodward & Maple, Birmingham, Michigan, and photographed by Yakov Faytlin on The Village Club second floor landing.

7

DESSERTS
Desserts

THE GOLD ROOM OF THE VILLAGE CLUB CIRCA 1961

The Gold Room was the sitting room for the adjacent Garden Room, one of the master bedrooms. It derives its name from the gold leaf ceiling. Although the Gold Room has gone through many decorating styles, the gold ceiling remains. The Garden and Gold Rooms are currently used as bride's rooms and for meetings, bridge, and small parties.

DOUBLE-CHOCOLATE MOUSSE CAKE

CAKE

16 ounces semisweet chocolate
2 cups (4 sticks) butter or margarine
1 cup sugar
1 cup half-and-half
1 tablespoon vanilla extract
1/2 teaspoon salt
8 eggs

CHOCOLATE GLAZE

1 cup semisweet chocolate pieces
2 tablespoons butter or margarine
3 tablespoons milk
2 tablespoons light corn syrup
1 cup heavy whipping cream

For the cake, combine the chocolate, butter, sugar, half-and-half, vanilla and salt in a 3-quart saucepan. Cook over low heat until the chocolate is melted and the mixture is smooth, stirring constantly. Beat the eggs lightly in a bowl. Beat in the chocolate mixture gradually. Pour into a greased 10-inch springform pan. Bake at 350 degrees for 45 minutes or until a wooden pick inserted 2 inches from the edge comes out clean. Remove to a wire rack to cool completely. Loosen from the side of the pan with a sharp knife and remove the side. Wrap the cake in plastic wrap and chill for at least 6 hours.

For the glaze, combine the chocolate and butter in a 2-quart saucepan. Cook over low heat until the chocolate is melted and the mixture is smooth, stirring constantly. Remove from the heat and beat in the milk and corn syrup. Place the cake on a cake plate lined with strips of waxed paper around the edge to catch drips. Spread the warm glaze over the cake with a metal spatula. Remove the waxed paper. Whip the cream in a bowl. Spoon into a pastry bag fitted with a medium star tip. Pipe the cream around the edge of the cake. Garnish with candied violets, if desired. Chill until ready to serve. *Serves 12.*

MOLTEN CHOCOLATE CAKES

14 ounces imported bittersweet or
semisweet chocolate, chopped
1¹/₄ cups (2¹/₂ sticks) unsalted butter
2 teaspoons coriander
2 teaspoons cardamom
1 teaspoon ground cinnamon
¹/₂ teaspoon ground cloves

¹/₂ teaspoon white pepper
6 eggs
6 egg yolks
2 teaspoons vanilla extract
3 cups confectioners' sugar
1 cup all-purpose flour
Confectioners' sugar

Combine the chocolate, butter, coriander, cardamom, cinnamon, cloves and white pepper in a heavy saucepan. Cook over low heat until the chocolate is melted and the mixture is smooth, stirring constantly. Remove from the heat and let cool slightly. Beat the eggs, egg yolks and vanilla lightly in a bowl. Whisk in 3 cups confectioners' sugar. Whisk in the chocolate mixture. Whisk in the flour. Pour the batter equally into eight generously buttered 12-ounce soufflé dishes.

Bake at 425 degrees for 15 to 18 minutes or until the batter rises above the tops of the soufflés dishes, the edges are dark brown and the centers are still soft and runny. Run a small knife around the edge to loosen the cakes. Let stand for 5 minutes. Invert each cake onto a serving plate. Dust with confectioners' sugar and serve with a scoop of rum raisin ice cream or your favorite ice cream. *Serves 8.*

APPLE AND NUT UPSIDE-DOWN CAKE

6 large apples, peeled, cored and
cut into eighths
1 teaspoon ground cinnamon
2 eggs
¹/₂ cup toasted chopped walnuts or pecans
³/₄ cup sugar

1 cup all-purpose flour
¹/₂ cup (1 stick) butter, melted
¹/₂ teaspoon lemon juice
1 teaspoon vanilla extract
Ground cinnamon

Spread the apples over the bottom of a greased 10-inch deep-dish pie plate or bundt pan. Sprinkle with 1 teaspoon cinnamon. Combine the eggs, walnuts, sugar, flour, melted butter, lemon juice and vanilla in a bowl and mix well.

Pour evenly over the apples. Sprinkle with cinnamon. Bake at 375 degrees for 45 minutes or until golden brown. Invert onto a serving plate and let cool. Serve with whipped cream or ice cream. *Serves 12 to 14.*

DECADENT BREAD PUDDING

1 cup Grand Marnier	1 cup sugar
1/4 cup water	1 tablespoon vanilla extract
6 eggs	1/2 teaspoon nutmeg
3 cups heavy cream	1 pound (about 8) croissants, torn into pieces
2 cups half-and-half	1 cup dried apricots, chopped

Simmer the liqueur and water in a heavy saucepan for 5 minutes. Remove from the heat and let cool completely. Whisk the eggs, cream, half-and-half, sugar, vanilla, nutmeg and liqueur mixture in a bowl. Toss the torn croissants with the dried apricots in a 9×13-inch baking dish and spread evenly over the bottom. Pour the cream mixture evenly over the croissants. Press the bread gently with a wooden spoon.

Let stand for 20 minutes. Cover the baking dish with foil. Place the baking dish in a larger baking pan. Add enough hot water to the larger pan to come 1 inch up the sides of the baking dish. Bake at 350 degrees for 1 hour. Remove the foil and bake for 30 minutes longer. Remove the baking dish carefully from the water to a wire rack to cool. *Serves 15.*

HOLIDAY CRANBERRY STEAMED PUDDING

1 1/2 cups fresh cranberries	1/2 cup (1 stick) butter
1/2 cup dark molasses	1 cup sugar
1 1/2 cups all-purpose flour	1/2 cup heavy cream
2 teaspoons baking soda	1 teaspoon vanilla extract
1/3 cup (or more) hot water	1/2 cup brandy, warmed

Combine the cranberries and molasses in a bowl and mix well. Stir in the flour. Combine the baking soda and hot water in a bowl and mix well. Stir into the cranberry mixture. Add an additional 2 teaspoons water, if needed to incorporate the flour. The batter will be stiff. Butter the top part of a double boiler and add the batter. Place over simmering water. Steam, covered, for 3 hours. Remove the top part of the double boiler to a wire rack and let stand for a few minutes.

Invert the pudding onto a heatproof serving plate. Melt 1/2 cup butter in a saucepan. Stir in the sugar, cream and vanilla. Cook until hot and the sugar is dissolved, stirring constantly. Pour into a heatproof pitcher. Pour the warm brandy over the warm pudding. Ignite the brandy with a long match. Serve with the sauce. *Serves 8.*

Note: This may also be steamed in pudding molds set on a trivet in a pan of hot water in the oven.

STICKY DATE PUDDING WITH CARAMEL SAUCE

PUDDING

1 (10-ounce) package pitted dates,
coarsely chopped (1^3/$_4$ cups)
2 cups water
1^1/$_2$ teaspoons baking soda
2 cups all-purpose flour
^{1}/$_2$ teaspoon baking powder
^{1}/$_2$ teaspoon ginger
^{1}/$_2$ teaspoon salt
6 tablespoons unsalted butter, softened
1 cup sugar
3 eggs

CARAMEL SAUCE

^{3}/$_4$ cup (1^1/$_2$ sticks) plus 2 tablespoons unsalted butter
1^1/$_3$ cups packed brown sugar
1 cup heavy cream
^{1}/$_2$ teaspoon vanilla extract

For the pudding, combine the dates and water in a 2-quart saucepan. Simmer for 5 minutes. Remove from the heat and stir in the baking soda. Let stand for 20 minutes. Sift the flour, baking powder, ginger and salt together. Beat the butter and sugar in a bowl until light and fluffy. Add the eggs one at a time, beating well after each addition. Add the dry ingredients in three batches, stirring just until mixed. Add the date mixture and mix well with a wooden spoon. Pour the batter into a buttered and floured 8×8-inch baking pan. Place the baking pan in a larger baking pan. Add enough hot water to the larger pan to come halfway up the sides of the smaller pan.

Bake at 375 degrees on the middle oven rack for 40 to 45 minutes or until a wooden pick inserted in the center comes out clean. Remove the smaller baking pan carefully from the water to a wire rack and let cool slightly.

For the sauce, melt the butter in a 1^1/$_2$- to 2-quart saucepan over medium heat. Stir in the brown sugar. Bring to a boil, stirring occasionally. Stir in the cream and vanilla. Simmer for 5 minutes or until slightly thickened. Remove from the heat and let cool slightly. Serve with squares of the warm pudding and top with vanilla ice cream, if desired. ***Serves 9.***

LEMON DELICACY

1/4 cup (1/2 stick) butter, softened
1 1/2 cups sugar
4 egg yolks
1/4 cup all-purpose flour
Juice of 2 lemons (about 6 tablespoons)
2 cups milk
4 egg whites

Beat the butter and sugar in a bowl until light and fluffy. Beat in the egg yolks. Beat in the flour. Beat in the lemon juice. Beat in the milk. Beat the egg whites in a bowl until stiff. Fold into the batter. Pour into a lightly buttered and floured 2-quart baking dish. Place the baking dish in a larger baking pan. Add enough hot water to the larger pan to come halfway up the sides of the baking dish.

Bake at 350 degrees for 1 hour and 5 minutes or until golden brown on top and soft inside. Check every 20 minutes and if getting too brown, loosely cover the top with foil.

Remove the baking dish carefully from the water to a wire rack to cool completely. Chill until cold. Serve in dessert or sherbet glasses and garnish with fresh berries, a sprig of mint and a cookie. *Serves 8 to 10.*

MOUSSE IN A MINUTE

A favorite from Food With A Flair

1 cup (6 ounces) miniature chocolate chips
2 eggs
3 tablespoons hot very strong coffee
1 to 2 tablespoons rum or orange-flavored liqueur
3/4 cup scalded milk

Combine the chocolate chips, eggs, coffee, rum and hot milk in a blender. Process at high speed for 2 minutes. Pour into four dessert cups. Chill until cold. Serve with whipped cream, chopped almonds and chocolate curls. *Serves 4.*

Note: If you are concerned about using raw eggs, use eggs pasteurized in their shells, which are sold at some specialty food stores, or use an equivalent amount of pasteurized egg substitute.

WHITE FOREST TORTE

9 egg whites
$1/4$ teaspoon cream of tartar
$2^1/4$ cups (scant) sugar
$1^1/2$ cups almonds, ground

2 tablespoons all-purpose flour
4 cups heavy whipping cream
$1/2$ cup sugar
1 teaspoon vanilla extract

Beat the egg whites, cream of tartar and $3/4$ cup of the sugar in a bowl until stiff peaks form. Fold in the remaining $1^1/2$ cups sugar, the almonds and flour. Pour into three waxed paper-lined 9-inch cake pans. Bake at 400 degrees for 18 to 20 minutes or until golden brown. Cool in the pans for 10 minutes.

Remove to a wire rack to cool. Remove the waxed paper. Whip the cream, $1/2$ cup sugar and the vanilla in a bowl until stiff. Spread evenly over each layer of the cake. Garnish with chocolate shavings and dust with confectioners' sugar. *Serves 8 to 10.*

FABULOUS RASPBERRY CHEESECAKE

2 cups graham cracker crumbs
$1/3$ cup sugar
$5^1/3$ tablespoons butter, melted
24 ounces cream cheese, softened
1 cup sugar
2 teaspoons vanilla extract
3 eggs

$1/2$ to 1 cup sour cream
$1/2$ cup raspberries, mashed
$1/3$ to $1/2$ cup sugar
$1/4$ cup water
$4^1/2$ teaspoons cornstarch
1 cup raspberries

Combine the graham cracker crumbs, $1/3$ cup sugar and the butter in a bowl and mix well. Press over the bottom and up the side of a 9- to 10-inch springform pan.

Beat the cream cheese in a bowl until light and fluffy. Beat in 1 cup sugar and the vanilla gradually. Add the eggs one at a time, beating well after each addition. Stir in the sour cream. Pour into the prepared crust. Bake at 350 degrees for 30 minutes; do not overbake. Remove to a wire rack to cool completely. Chill, covered, until cold.

Combine $1/2$ cup mashed raspberries, $1/3$ to $1/2$ cup sugar, the water and cornstarch in a saucepan and mix well. Cook until thickened, stirring constantly. Remove from the heat and let cool to room temperature. Fold in 1 cup raspberries. Spread over the top of the cheesecake. Chill, covered, until serving time. Loosen from the side of the pan with a sharp knife and remove the side. *Serves 16.*

HOLLYWOOD'S FAVORITE CHEESECAKE

1¹/₄ cups zwieback cracker crumbs or
graham cracker crumbs
¹/₄ cup sugar
¹/₄ teaspoon ground cinnamon
¹/₄ cup (¹/₂ stick) butter, melted
24 ounces cream cheese, softened

¹/₂ teaspoon salt
1 tablespoon vanilla extract
4 egg whites, at room temperature
1 cup sugar
2 cups sour cream
2 tablespoons sugar

Combine the cracker crumbs, ¹/₄ cup sugar, the cinnamon and melted butter in a bowl and mix well. Press over the bottom and up the side of a 9-inch springform pan. Chill until cold.

Beat the cream cheese, salt and vanilla in a bowl until light and fluffy. Beat the egg whites in a bowl until foamy. Beat in 1 cup sugar 2 tablespoons at a time until soft peaks form. Fold the cream cheese mixture gently into the egg white mixture. Pour into the prepared crust.

Bake at 350 degrees for 25 minutes. Remove to a wire rack. Combine the sour cream and 2 tablespoons sugar in a bowl and mix well. Spread gently over the top of the cheesecake. Bake at 450 degrees for 4 to 5 minutes. Open the oven door but do not remove the cheesecake for 1 hour. Remove to a wire rack to cool completely. Chill, covered, for at least 24 hours. Loosen from the side of the pan with a sharp knife and remove the side. Serve with fresh strawberries or other fresh fruit. *Serves 16.*

EASY OREO ICE CREAM

3 egg yolks
1 (14-ounce) can sweetened condensed milk
2 tablespoons water

4 teaspoons vanilla extract
1 cup coarsely crushed Oreo cookies
2 cups heavy whipping cream, whipped

Beat the egg yolks in a bowl. Stir in the sweetened condensed milk, water and vanilla. Fold in the crushed cookies and whipped cream. Spoon into a foil-lined 5×9-inch loaf pan or 2-quart freezer container. Freeze, covered, for 6 hours or until firm. Invert onto a cutting board, remove the foil and cut into slices or scoop from the container. *Serves 10 to 12.*

Note: If you are concerned about using raw eggs, use eggs pasteurized in their shells, which are sold at some specialty food stores, or use an equivalent amount of pasteurized egg substitute.

FROZEN LEMON CREAM

1 cup milk
1 cup heavy cream
1 cup sugar
Grated zest and juice of 2 lemons

Combine the milk, cream and sugar in a bowl and stir until the sugar is dissolved. Pour into a 9×13-inch baking pan. Freeze until slushy. Remove from the freezer. Beat in the lemon zest and lemon juice.

Freeze for 2 hours. Remove from the freezer and beat well. Freeze until solid. May be served in hollowed out lemons. Garnish with mint leaves. *Serves 4 to 6.*

ICE CREAM PIE SPECTACULAR

2 egg whites
$1/8$ teaspoon cream of tartar
$1/8$ teaspoon salt
$1/2$ cup granulated sugar
$1/2$ cup finely chopped nuts
$1/2$ teaspoon vanilla extract
1 pint coffee ice cream, softened

1 pint (or more) vanilla ice cream, softened
3 tablespoons butter
1 cup packed light brown sugar
$1/2$ cup heavy cream
$1/2$ cup golden raisins
1 teaspoon vanilla extract

Beat the egg whites, cream of tartar and salt in a bowl until foamy. Beat in the granulated sugar gradually until very stiff peaks form. Fold in the nuts and $1/2$ teaspoon vanilla. Spread over the bottom and up the side of a buttered 9-inch pie plate. Bake at 300 degrees for 50 to 55 minutes. Remove to a wire rack to cool completely. Spread the coffee ice cream into the cooled crust. Spread the vanilla ice cream over the coffee ice cream. Freeze until firm.

Melt the butter in a saucepan. Add the brown sugar. Cook for 10 minutes or until smooth, stirring constantly. Remove from the heat and stir in the cream gradually. Return to the heat and cook for 1 minute. Stir in the raisins and 1 teaspoon vanilla. Serve warm or chilled with slices of the pie. *Serves 8.*

PRALINE ICE CREAM PIE WITH CARAMEL SAUCE

1¹/₂ tablespoons butter, softened
1¹/₂ cups flaked coconut
1 quart butter pecan ice cream, softened
1 quart chocolate chip ice cream, softened
Butterscotch caramel ice cream topping

Spread the butter over the bottom and up the side of a 10-inch glass pie plate. Press the coconut evenly onto the butter. Bake at 300 degrees for 13 minutes or until light brown. Remove to a wire rack to cool completely. Spread the butter pecan ice cream into the cooled crust. Cover with plastic wrap.

Freeze for 2 hours or until firm. Remove the plastic wrap and top with small scoops of the chocolate chip ice cream. Cover with plastic wrap and freeze until firm or up to 1 month. Cut into slices and place on serving plates. Drizzle each slice with butterscotch caramel topping. *Serves 8.*

FIG COMPOTE WITH HONEY AND THYME

3 cups water
³/₄ cup honey
³/₄ cup sugar
2 teaspoons thyme
1 pound dried figs, stems removed

Combine the water, honey, sugar and thyme in a saucepan. Bring to a boil and reduce the heat. Add the figs. Simmer for 10 minutes or until the figs are softened. Remove the figs to a bowl with a slotted spoon. Increase the heat to high. Boil until the liquid is reduced to 1 cup.

Remove from the heat and let cool slightly. Pour over the figs and let cool to room temperature. Serve for dessert with cheese and other fruits. *Serves 8.*

Note: This can be stored, covered, in the refrigerator for up to 2 weeks.

BAKED MANCHEGO CHEESE
WITH PEAR COMPOTE AND SLICED PEARS

PEAR COMPOTE

4 teaspoons vegetable oil
2 tablespoons finely chopped red bell pepper
1/4 teaspoon dry mustard
Pinch of salt
4 pears, peeled, cored and chopped
Pinch of ground allspice
Pinch of ginger
Pinch of ground cloves
1 tablespoon (heaping) golden raisins
1/4 cup apple cider vinegar
1/4 cup packed light brown sugar

CHEESE

1/2 cup unblanched whole almonds, ground
1/2 cup panko (Japanese bread crumbs)
1/2 teaspoon salt
1 egg
16 ounces Manchego cheese, rind removed and cheese cut into 16 equal wedges
Sliced almonds
2 pears, cored and thinly sliced

For the compote, heat the oil in a small skillet. Add the bell pepper, dry mustard and salt and sauté for 5 minutes. Add the pears, allspice, ginger and cloves and sauté for 1 to 2 minutes. Stir in the raisins, vinegar and brown sugar. Bring to a boil. Cook until the pears have softened and the mixture is the texture of chunky applesauce. Chill, covered, until cold.

For the cheese, combine the almonds, panko and salt in a flat shallow dish. Beat the egg in a flat shallow dish.

Dip each cheese wedge in the egg and then coat in the panko mixture. Place in a Silpat-lined or baking parchment-lined 10×15-inch baking pan. Spray each wedge with nonstick cooking spray. Bake at 400 degrees for 5 to 7 minutes or just until the cheese is softened. Place two cheese wedges at a right angle on each of eight desserts plates. Top each with about 1 tablespoon of the compote and sprinkle with sliced almonds. Arrange pear slices next to the cheese. Serve with water biscuits or baguette slices. *Serves 8.*

PEARS POACHED IN SPICED RED WINE

6 firm pears, peeled
Juice of 1 lemon
1 cup red wine
$^1/_4$ cup sugar

$^1/_4$ cup currants
1 vanilla bean, or 1 teaspoon vanilla extract
6 whole cloves

Stand the pears upright in a saucepan. Squeeze the lemon juice over the pears. Pour the wine over the pears and sprinkle the sugar over the top. Add the currants, vanilla bean and cloves to the wine. Simmer, covered, for 20 minutes or until the pears are tender but still firm.

Turn the pears on their sides halfway through cooking and baste several times with the wine mixture. Remove to serving bowls and spoon some of the wine and currants over each. Garnish with lemon zest strips and serve with a scoop of vanilla ice cream, if desired. *Serves 6.*

POACHED PEARS WITH CINNAMON ICE CREAM AND STRAWBERRY RASPBERRY COULIS

3 large firm Anjou or Bartlett pears
2 cups dry white wine
$^1/_4$ cup sugar
$^1/_2$ teaspoon vanilla extract
1 cinnamon stick

1 (2-inch) piece lemon zest
$^3/_4$ cup strawberry raspberry preserves, (strained, if desired)
1 pint cinnamon, caramel or vanilla ice cream
2 tablespoons chopped pistachios

Peel the pears and cut into halves lengthwise. Core the pears and cut a thin slice off the outside of each half so they will lay flat. Combine the wine, sugar, vanilla, cinnamon stick and lemon zest in a 10-inch skillet and bring to a boil. Add the pears cored side up. Add enough water to cover the pears. Reduce the heat and simmer for 20 minutes or until tender. Remove the pears to dessert plates with a slotted spoon and let cool. Cook the poaching liquid over high heat until reduced to $^1/_3$ cup.

Remove from the heat. Remove and discard the cinnamon stick and lemon zest. Stir in the preserves. Place a scoop of ice cream on each pear half. Drizzle the sauce over and around each pear half. Sprinkle with the pistachios. *Serves 6.*

Note: You may use a combination of strawberry and raspberry preserves if strawberry raspberry preserves are not available.

RHUBARB SQUARES

2 cups all-purpose flour
1 teaspoon baking soda
1/2 teaspoon salt
1 1/2 cups packed brown sugar
1/2 cup shortening
1 egg

1 cup sour cream
1 1/2 cups chopped rhubarb (1/2-inch pieces)
1/2 cup granulated sugar
1/2 cup chopped walnuts
1 teaspoon ground cinnamon
1 tablespoon margarine, melted

Mix the flour, baking soda and salt. Beat the brown sugar, shortening and egg in a bowl until light and fluffy. Beat in the dry ingredients alternately with the sour cream. Stir in the rhubarb. Spoon into a greased and floured 9×13-inch baking pan.

Mix the granulated sugar, walnuts, cinnamon and melted margarine in a bowl until crumbly. Sprinkle over the rhubarb mixture. Bake at 350 degrees for 30 to 40 minutes or until a wooden pick inserted in the center comes out clean. Remove to a wire rack. Serve warm with ice cream or serve plain at room temperature. *Serves 15.*

STRAWBERRY PAVLOVA

4 or 5 egg whites
1 to 1 1/4 cups sugar
2 teaspoons cornstarch
1 teaspoon vanilla extract
1 teaspoon white vinegar

1 cup heavy whipping cream, whipped
3 or 4 kiwifruit, peeled and sliced
1 quart fresh strawberries, sliced
1 pint fresh blueberries

Beat the egg whites in a bowl until stiff peaks form. Beat in 1/4 cup sugar per egg white gradually. Beat in the cornstarch just until blended. Beat in the vanilla and vinegar. Spread to an 8-inch circle on a foil-lined baking sheet. Mound the outside edge to make a slight wall. Bake at 300 degrees for 1 hour. Turn off the oven.

Leave in the oven overnight without opening the oven door. Remove the baked meringue to a serving platter. Spread with the whipped cream. Arrange the sliced kiwifruit around the outside edge and the sliced strawberries in the middle. Sprinkle the blueberries over the top. Chill until ready to serve. *Serves 6 to 8.*

FRUIT SALSA SUNDAES

1/3 cup seedless strawberry or raspberry
fruit spread
2 tablespoons finely chopped
crystallized ginger
1 tablespoon hot water

1 cup chopped papaya, peaches or nectarines
6 ounces fresh raspberries (about 1 cup)
6 ounces fresh blueberries (about 1 cup)
6 (1/2-cup) scoops vanilla ice cream or
frozen yogurt

Combine the fruit spread, ginger and hot water in a bowl and mix well. Add the papaya, raspberries and blueberries and toss gently. Chill, covered, for up to 8 hours.

Spoon a small amount of the fruit mixture into each of six sundae glasses. Top each with a scoop of ice cream. Spoon the remaining fruit mixture over the ice cream. Garnish with a sprig of mint. *Serves 6.*

SPLENDID FRUIT CRISP

3 cups frozen sliced rhubarb, thawed, drained
and patted dry, or chopped fresh rhubarb
1 tablespoon all-purpose flour
1 (10-ounce) package frozen blueberries
1 tablespoon all-purpose flour
1 (7-ounce) package frozen raspberries
1 tablespoon all-purpose flour
1/2 cup golden raisins
1 cup seedless green grapes

4 cups sliced cored peeled apples
1/2 cup chopped walnuts
1 (14-ounce) can peaches, drained and chopped
1/2 cup packed brown sugar
1/2 teaspoon ground cinnamon
10 2/3 tablespoons butter, softened
1 cup packed brown sugar
1 1/4 cups all-purpose flour
1/2 teaspoon ground cinnamon

Spread the rhubarb over the bottom of a lightly buttered 9×13-inch baking dish. Sprinkle with 1 tablespoon flour. Spread the blueberries over the rhubarb and sprinkle with 1 tablespoon flour. Spread the raspberries over the blueberries and sprinkle with 1 tablespoon flour. Sprinkle the raisins and grapes over the raspberries. Arrange the apple slices over the grapes and sprinkle with the walnuts. Spread the peaches over the walnuts.

Combine 1/2 cup brown sugar and 1/2 teaspoon cinnamon in a bowl and mix well. Sprinkle over the peaches. Beat the butter and 1 cup brown sugar in a bowl until creamy. Stir in 1 1/4 cups flour and 1/2 teaspoon cinnamon gradually. Mix with hands until crumbly. Sprinkle evenly over all the fruit. Bake at 350 degrees for 55 to 60 minutes or until the apples are tender. Let stand for 10 minutes before serving. *Serves 12 to 16.*

BLACK RUSSIAN CAKE

1 (2-layer) package yellow cake mix
1 (3-ounce) package chocolate instant
pudding mix
1/2 cup instant coffee granules
4 eggs

1/2 cup canola oil
1/4 cup vodka
3/4 cup coffee liqueur
Confectioners' sugar

Combine the cake mix, pudding mix and coffee granules in a bowl and mix well. Add the eggs, canola oil, vodka and coffee liqueur. Beat with an electric mixer for at least 2 minutes. Pour into a large nonstick bundt pan. Bake at 325 degrees for 50 to 60 minutes or until the cake tests done. Remove to a wire rack to cool completely.

Invert onto a cake plate and dust with confectioners' sugar. Serve with ice cream, if desired. **Serves 12 to 14.**

Note: *Feel free to use the least expensive vodka and coffee liqueur. This cake keeps at room temperature for days. It freezes well and travels well.*

BLUEBERRY POUND CAKE

3 cups all-purpose flour
2 cups fresh or frozen blueberries
1 teaspoon baking powder
1/2 teaspoon baking soda
1/2 teaspoon salt
2 cups granulated sugar
1/2 cup (1 stick) light butter, softened

4 ounces reduced-fat cream cheese, softened
3 eggs
1 egg white
8 ounces low-fat lemon yogurt
2 teaspoons vanilla extract
1/2 cup confectioners' sugar
4 teaspoons lemon juice

Remove 2 tablespoons of the flour to a bowl. Add the blueberries and toss to coat. Combine the remaining flour, baking powder, baking soda and salt and mix well. Combine the granulated sugar, butter and cream cheese in a bowl. Beat with an electric mixer at medium speed for 5 minutes. Add the eggs and egg white one at a time, beating well after each addition. Beat in the dry ingredients alternately with the yogurt, beginning and ending with the dry ingredients.

Fold in the blueberries and vanilla. Pour into a 10-inch tube pan sprayed with nonstick cooking spray. Bake at 350 degrees for 1 hour and 10 minutes or until a wooden pick inserted in the center comes out clean. Cool in the pan for 10 minutes. Invert onto a serving plate. Combine the confectioners' sugar and lemon juice in a bowl and mix well. Drizzle the glaze over the warm cake. Cut the cake with a serrated knife. **Serves 16.**

GETTY MUSEUM CARROT CAKE

1 (8-ounce) can crushed pineapple, drained
1¹/2 cups corn oil
2 cups granulated sugar
3 eggs
2 cups all-purpose flour
2 teaspoons each ground cinnamon and baking soda
1 teaspoon salt

2 teaspoons vanilla extract
2 cups shredded carrots
1 cup chopped walnuts
3 ounces cream cheese, softened
¹/2 cup (1 stick) margarine, softened
1¹/4 cups confectioners' sugar
¹/4 cup chopped walnuts

Remove ¹/4 cup crushed pineapple and set aside. Combine the remaining pineapple, corn oil, granulated sugar, eggs, flour, cinnamon, baking soda, salt, vanilla, carrots and 1 cup walnuts in a bowl and mix well. Pour into a greased 9×13-inch cake pan. Bake at 350 degrees for 1 hour or until the cake tests done. Remove to a wire rack to cool.

Beat the cream cheese, margarine and confectioners' sugar in a bowl until light and fluffy. Stir in the reserved ¹/4 cup crushed pineapple and ¹/4 cup walnuts. Spread over the top of the cooled cake. *Serves 14.*

Note: You may also use a greased tube or bundt pan for this cake.

GINGER CAKE IN A BLACKENED SKILLET

¹/2 cup each port and golden raisins
1¹/2 cups unbleached flour
1 cup sugar
2 teaspoons ginger
1 teaspoon ground cinnamon
¹/2 cup shortening

³/4 cup (about) buttermilk
1 teaspoon baking soda
¹/2 teaspoon salt
1 egg, beaten
3 tablespoons dark molasses
¹/2 cup toasted chopped walnuts

Bring the port to a boil in a saucepan over medium-high heat. Add the raisins and simmer for 1 minute. Remove from the heat and allow the raisins to soak. Combine the flour, sugar, ginger and cinnamon in a large bowl and mix well. Cut in the shortening with a pastry blender or fork until crumbly. Drain the port into a 2-cup liquid measuring cup, reserving the raisins. Add enough buttermilk to the port to make 1 cup.

Add the baking soda and salt to the buttermilk mixture and stir until the salt is dissolved. Add to the flour mixture. Add the egg and molasses and mix well; the batter may be lumpy. Stir in the raisins and walnuts. Pour into a well-greased 10-inch cast-iron skillet. Bake at 350 degrees for 50 minutes or until the cake tests done. Remove to a wire rack. Cut into wedges and serve warm with whipped cream. *Serves 12 to 16.*

LUSCIOUS LEMON CAKE

CAKE
3 cups cake flour
1 teaspoon baking powder
1/4 teaspoon salt
1 cup (2 sticks) butter, softened
2 cups sugar
3 eggs
1 cup buttermilk
Grated zest of 1 lemon
3 tablespoons lemon juice

LEMON GLAZE
1/4 cup (1/2 stick) butter, softened
1 1/2 cups confectioners' sugar
1/4 cup lemon juice

For the cake, mix the flour, baking powder and salt together. Beat the butter and sugar in a bowl until light and fluffy. Add the eggs one at a time, beating well after each addition. Beat in the dry ingredients alternately with the buttermilk, beginning and ending with the dry ingredients. Beat in the lemon zest and lemon juice. Pour into a nonstick tube pan sprayed with nonstick cooking spray.

Bake at 300 degrees for 50 minutes or until a wooden pick inserted in the center comes out clean. Cool in the pan for 10 minutes. Invert onto a serving plate.

For the glaze, combine the butter, confectioners' sugar and lemon juice in a bowl and mix well. Drizzle over the warm cake. Serve the cake with fresh strawberries or a dessert wine. ***Serves 12.***

PUMPKIN CAKE ROLL

3/4 cup all-purpose flour
1 teaspoon baking powder
2 teaspoons ground cinnamon
1 1/2 teaspoons nutmeg
1 teaspoon ginger
1/2 teaspoon salt
3 eggs
1 cup granulated sugar

2/3 cup canned pumpkin
1 teaspoon lemon juice
1 cup finely chopped walnuts
Confectioners' sugar
6 ounces cream cheese, softened
1/4 cup (1/2 stick) butter
1 cup confectioners' sugar
1/2 teaspoon vanilla extract

Mix the flour, baking powder, cinnamon, nutmeg, ginger and salt together. Beat the eggs in a bowl with an electric mixer at high speed for 5 minutes. Beat in the granulated sugar gradually. Stir in the pumpkin and lemon juice. Fold in the dry ingredients. Spread in a well-greased and floured 10×15-inch cake pan. Sprinkle with the walnuts. Bake at 375 degrees for 15 minutes or until the cake tests done. Loosen the edges of the cake.

Invert onto a clean kitchen towel dusted generously with confectioners' sugar. Roll the warm cake in the towel as for a jelly roll from the short side and place on a wire rack to cool. Unroll the cooled cake carefully and remove the towel. Combine the cream cheese, butter, 1 cup confectioners' sugar and the vanilla in a bowl and beat well. Spread over the cooled cake and reroll. Wrap in plastic wrap and chill. Slice when ready to serve. *Serves 8.*

PECAN DATE PIE

2 eggs
1 cup sugar
1/2 cup chopped dates
1/2 cup (1 stick) butter, melted

1/2 cup chopped pecans
1/2 cup flaked coconut
1/2 teaspoon vinegar
1 unbaked (9-inch) pie shell

Beat the eggs and sugar in a bowl. Stir in the dates. Stir in the melted butter. Add the pecans, coconut and vinegar and mix well. Pour into the pie shell. Place in a 325-degree oven.

Reduce the oven temperature to 300 degrees. Bake for 45 minutes. Remove to a wire rack to cool completely. Chill, covered, overnight. Serve with whipped cream, if desired. *Serves 8.*

SUMMER BLUEBERRY RASPBERRY PIE

6 ounces cream cheese, softened
Sugar to taste
1 baked (9- or 10-inch) pie shell
2 tablespoons cornstarch
$1/2$ cup sugar
6 tablespoons water
2 cups fresh blueberries
1 tablespoon fresh lemon juice
$1^1/2$ cups fresh blueberries
1 cup fresh raspberries
$1/2$ cup fresh blueberries

Combine the cream cheese and a small amount of sugar in a bowl and mix well. Spread over the bottom of the pie shell. Combine the cornstarch and $1/2$ cup sugar in a saucepan and mix well. Stir in the water and 2 cups blueberries. Bring to a boil.

Simmer for 2 minutes. Remove from the heat and stir in the lemon juice and $1^1/2$ cups blueberries. Let cool slightly. Pour into the prepared pie shell. Sprinkle the raspberries and $1/2$ cup blueberries over the top. *Serves 6 to 8.*

To keep berries fresh longer, don't wash them immediately after bringing them home; even a gentle rinse crushes and bruises berries, spoiling them faster. Instead, put them in a colander and store them in the refrigerator until ready to use.

UNHUMBLE RASPBERRY CHOCOLATE PIE

1 cup all-purpose flour
1/4 cup packed brown sugar
1/2 cup (1 stick) butter, softened
1/2 cup chopped pecans or walnuts
1/2 cup (1 stick) butter, softened
1/2 cup sugar
2 ounces unsweetened chocolate, melted and cooled
2 eggs
1 cup heavy whipping cream, whipped
10 to 12 ounces frozen raspberries, thawed,
drained and juice reserved
1/3 cup currant jelly
1 tablespoon cornstarch
2 tablespoons water
2 tablespoons crème de cassis

Mix the flour, brown sugar and 1/2 cup butter in a bowl until crumbly. Stir in the pecans. Spread over the bottom of a 9×13-inch baking pan. Bake at 400 degrees for 10 to 15 minutes, stirring frequently to avoid burning. Remove to a wire rack and cool slightly. Press the mixture over the bottom and up the side of a 9-inch pie plate. Chill until cold.

Combine 1/2 cup butter and the granulated sugar in a bowl. Beat with an electric mixer until light and fluffy. Stir in the cooled chocolate. Add the eggs one at a time, beating for 2 minutes after each addition. Fold in the whipped cream and drained raspberries. Spoon into the prepared crust, mounding the outside edge to make a slight wall. Chill for at least 2 hours.

Heat the jelly and reserved raspberry juice in a saucepan. Dissolve the cornstarch in the water in a small bowl. Add to the jelly mixture. Bring to a boil and reduce the heat. Simmer until thickened, stirring constantly. Remove from the heat and stir in the liqueur. Let cool to room temperature. Pour the sauce over the center of the pie and garnish with pecan halves. *Serves 8 to 10.*

Note: This is a rich dessert and the servings should be small.

If you are concerned about using raw eggs, use eggs pasteurized in their shells, which are sold at some specialty food stores, or use an equivalent amount of pasteurized egg substitute.

TARTE TATIN

$^1/_2$ cup (1 stick) unsalted butter
1 cup sugar
6 to 8 Granny Smith or Jonathan apples,
peeled, cored and quartered
1$^1/_2$ cups all-purpose flour
7 tablespoons unsalted butter, softened and
cut into pieces
1 egg
1 tablespoon sugar
Pinch of salt
1 to 2 tablespoons water

Melt $^1/_2$ cup butter in a 12-inch cast-iron skillet over medium-high heat. Sprinkle 1 cup sugar over the melted butter. Cook until the sugar is melted, stirring frequently. Place the apples in a circular pattern on top of the sugar mixture. Cook for 20 minutes, stirring carefully occasionally and keeping the apples in place. Increase the heat to high. Cook for 10 minutes or until the apples are golden brown on the bottom, watching carefully so that the apples don't burn. Remove from the heat.

Make a well in the flour in a bowl. Add 7 tablespoons butter, the egg, 1 tablespoon sugar and the salt to the well. Mix with your hands until crumbly. Mix in the water gradually to form a dough. Knead to mix well. Shape into a ball and flatten slightly. Chill, wrapped in plastic wrap, for 10 minutes. Roll into a 12$^1/_2$-inch circle on a lightly floured work surface. Press over the top of the skillet, tucking the edges inside the skillet. Bake at 425 degrees for 20 minutes or until golden brown. Invert immediately onto a serving plate. Serve warm with a dollop of crème fraîche or whipped cream. ***Serves 10.***

TORTA DI LEMONE

2 thin-skinned lemons, thinly sliced and seeded
5 eggs
1 cup sugar
1 1/2 cups lightly toasted walnuts
1 1/4 cups all-purpose flour
1/4 cup sugar

1/2 cup (1 stick) unsalted butter, softened
2 tablespoons lightly beaten egg
1/4 cup all-purpose flour
1 cup sugar
1/2 cup (1 stick) chilled unsalted butter, cut into small pieces

Purée the lemon slices in a food processor. Add five eggs one at a time with the processor running. Add 1 cup sugar and process until mixed. Remove to a bowl. Chill, covered, for 8 hours to overnight.

Grind the walnuts in a food processor. Add 1 1/4 cups flour and 1/4 cup sugar and process until mixed. Add 1/2 cup butter and 2 tablespoons egg and pulse just until the mixture forms a dough. Press over the bottom and up the side of a 9-inch fluted tart pan with a removable side. Chill for 1 hour to overnight.

Combine 1/4 cup flour, 1 cup sugar and 1/2 cup butter in a bowl and mix until crumbly.

Pour the chilled filling into the prepared crust. Sprinkle evenly with the flour mixture. Bake at 350 degrees on the middle oven rack for 40 to 45 minutes or until the topping is golden brown. Remove to a wire rack to cool slightly. Loosen from the side of the pan with a sharp knife and remove the side. Serve warm with whipped cream or mascarpone cheese. *Serves 8.*

A common misconception is that dessert wines match dessert. This is possible, but most dessert wines should be served in place of dessert. Dessert wines that pair up nicely include the following: Portuguese tawny port is great with apple and pear desserts; tawny ports from Australia work well with cheesecake; and ruby ports lean into dark chocolate and cherries. Try Moscato D'Asti with stone fruits and non-chocolate cakes and pastries. Vin Santo loves to have biscotti dipped into it. But the best use of dessert wines is after dessert and before coffee. Try Stilton or Valdeon cheese with walnuts or almonds with your favorite dessert wine.

BUTTER TART SQUARES

1¹/4 cups all-purpose flour
¹/4 cup packed brown sugar
¹/2 cup (1 stick) butter, softened
5¹/3 tablespoons butter, melted
2 tablespoons heavy cream

1 teaspoon vanilla extract
1 cup packed brown sugar
1 tablespoon all-purpose flour
1 egg, beaten
1 cup raisins

Combine 1¹/4 cups flour, the brown sugar and softened butter in a bowl and mix until crumbly. Press over the bottom of a 9×9-inch baking pan. Bake at 350 degrees for 10 minutes.

Combine the melted butter, cream, vanilla, brown sugar, 1 tablespoon flour, the egg and raisins in a bowl and mix well. Pour over the hot crust. Bake at 350 degrees for 20 to 30 minutes or until golden brown. Remove to a wire rack to cool. Cut into squares. *Makes 2 dozen squares.*

GOOD AND EASY BROWNIES

1 (19-ounce) package fudge brownie mix
¹/2 cup canola oil
2 eggs

¹/4 cup Kahlúa, or to taste
1¹/2 cups (9 ounces) semisweet chocolate chips
1 cup chopped pecans or walnuts

Combine the brownie mix, canola oil, eggs and Kahlúa in a bowl and mix well. Stir in the chocolate chips and pecans. Pour into a buttered 9×9-inch or 8×8-inch baking pan. Bake at 350 degrees for 35 to 40 minutes.

Brownies are done when they are slightly puffed and a wooden pick inserted in the center comes out almost clean; do not overbake. Remove to a wire rack to cool. *Makes 2 dozen brownies.*

Roasting enhances the flavor of nuts. Coat 1 cup of nuts evenly with 1 teaspoon vegetable oil. Spread the nuts evenly in a baking pan. Roast at 350 degrees for 5 to 10 minutes or until the nuts are fragrant and light brown, stirring occasionally; do not overcook.

GRASSHOPPER BARS

BARS
1^1/$_2$ cups sifted all-purpose flour
2 cups sugar
^{3}/$_4$ cup plus 2 tablespoons chocolate drink mix
1^1/$_2$ teaspoons salt
1 teaspoon baking powder
1^1/$_3$ cups (2 sticks plus 5^1/$_3$ tablespoons)
butter, softened
4 eggs
2 tablespoons light corn syrup
2 teaspoons vanilla extract
2 cups coarsely chopped nuts

CHOCOLATE MINT FROSTING
2 cups sifted confectioners' sugar
^{1}/$_4$ cup (^{1}/$_2$ stick) butter, softened
2 tablespoons milk
1 teaspoon mint extract
1^1/$_2$ ounces unsweetened chocolate
1^1/$_2$ tablespoons butter

For the bars, sift the flour, sugar, drink mix, salt and baking powder into a bowl. Add the butter, eggs, corn syrup and vanilla and mix well. Stir in the nuts. Spread in a greased 9×13-inch baking pan. Bake at 350 degrees for 40 to 45 minutes. Remove to a wire rack to cool completely.

For the frosting, combine the confectioners' sugar, butter, milk and mint extract in a bowl and beat well. Spread over the baked layer and let stand until firm. Melt the chocolate and butter in a small saucepan over low heat, stirring until smooth. Pour evenly over the frosting and let cool. Cut into bars. ***Makes 4 dozen bars.***

INVENTORY BARS

A favorite recipe from a past president

1 cup packed brown sugar
1/2 cup chopped walnuts
1/4 cup all-purpose flour
1 tablespoon ground cinnamon
2 tablespoons butter, melted
2 cups all-purpose flour
1 teaspoon baking soda
1/2 teaspoon baking powder
1 cup granulated sugar

1 cup water
1 cup raisins
1/2 cup (1 stick) butter
1 teaspoon ground cinnamon
1/2 teaspoon ground cloves
1/4 teaspoon nutmeg
1/4 teaspoon salt
1 teaspoon vanilla extract

Combine the brown sugar, walnuts, 1/4 cup flour, 1 tablespoon cinnamon and the melted butter in a bowl and mix until crumbly.

Mix the flour, baking soda and baking powder together. Mix the granulated sugar, water, raisins, 1/2 cup butter, 1 teaspoon cinnamon, the cloves, nutmeg and salt in a 2-quart saucepan. Bring to a boil and boil gently for 3 minutes, stirring occasionally.

Remove from the heat and let cool. Add the baking soda mixture and vanilla and mix well. Spread in a greased 10×15-inch baking pan. Sprinkle evenly with the brown sugar mixture.

Bake at 350 degrees for 20 to 25 minutes. Remove to a wire rack to cool. Cut into bars. *Makes 3 dozen bars.*

IMPERIAL SQUARES

1 cup (2 sticks) butter, softened
1 cup sugar
1/2 teaspoon baking soda

1 1/2 cups all-purpose flour
1/2 teaspoon vinegar

Beat the butter, sugar and baking soda in a bowl until light and fluffy. Beat in the flour and vinegar. Spread in a greased 10×15-inch baking pan.

Bake at 300 degrees for 20 to 30 minutes. Cut into squares while warm. Let stand until cool. Sprinkle with confectioners' sugar and chopped nuts, if desired. *Makes 3 to 4 dozen squares.*

LEMON CORNMEAL SHORTBREAD BARS

2 cups unbleached all-purpose flour
1 cup yellow cornmeal
1/2 teaspoon salt
1 1/2 cups (3 sticks) unsalted butter, softened

1 3/4 cups confectioners' sugar
1 tablespoon grated lemon zest
1 teaspoon vanilla extract

Whisk the flour, cornmeal and salt in a bowl. Combine the butter, confectioners' sugar, lemon zest and vanilla in a mixing bowl. Beat with the paddle attachment of an electric mixer at medium-high speed for 3 to 4 minutes or until light and fluffy. Add the dry ingredients and beat at low speed until a dough forms. Butter a 9×12-inch baking pan lightly and line the bottom with baking parchment.

Place the dough in the prepared baking pan. Press the dough evenly over the bottom of the pan using a rubber spatula or lightly floured fingers. Dip the tip of a knife into flour and score the dough to mark 45 bars. Bake at 325 degrees on the middle oven rack for 35 to 40 minutes or until golden brown. Remove to a wire rack and cut into bars. Let stand until cool. *Makes 45 bars.*

TRIPLE-CHOCOLATE BISCOTTI

1 3/4 cups all-purpose flour
1/3 cup baking cocoa
2 teaspoons baking powder
1/2 teaspoon salt
6 tablespoons unsalted butter, softened

1 cup sugar
3 eggs
1 1/2 teaspoons vanilla extract
1 1/3 cups (8 ounces) semisweet chocolate chips
1/2 cup (3 ounces) white chocolate chips

Sift the flour, baking cocoa, baking powder and salt together. Combine the butter and sugar in a bowl. Beat with an electric mixer until light and fluffy. Add the eggs one at a time, beating well after each addition. Beat in the vanilla. Beat in the dry ingredients. Stir in the semisweet chocolate chips and white chocolate chips. Drop the dough by heaping tablespoonfuls onto a baking parchment-lined cookie sheet in two 10- to 11-inch long strips, spacing 3 inches apart. Shape each strip into a 2 1/2×11-inch log using wet fingers.

Chill for 30 minutes. Bake at 350 degrees for 25 minutes or until the tops are dry and cracked and a wooden pick inserted in the center comes out clean. Cool on the cookie sheet for 10 minutes. Slide the logs carefully onto a cutting board. Cut gently with a serrated knife into 3/4-inch slices. Arrange upright on a cookie sheet lined with a clean piece of baking parchment. Bake at 300 degrees for 8 to 10 minutes or just until dry. Cool on the baking sheet. *Makes 2 to 3 dozen biscotti.*

PECAN AND GINGER BISCOTTI

$1^3/_4$ cups sifted all-purpose flour
$1/_2$ teaspoon baking powder
$1/_4$ teaspoon salt
$1/_2$ cup (1 stick) unsalted butter, softened
1 teaspoon vanilla extract
$1^1/_2$ cups sugar
4 eggs
3 cups pecan halves
5 ounces crystallized ginger, cut into small pieces
Bread crumbs

Sift the flour, baking powder and salt together. Place the butter in a bowl and beat with an electric mixer until light and fluffy. Beat in the vanilla and sugar. Add the eggs one at a time, beating well after each addition. Add the dry ingredients. Beat at low speed until mixed. Stir in the pecans and ginger. Butter two 4×8-inch loaf pans. Coat generously with bread crumbs, tapping out any excess. Spoon half the batter into each prepared pan, smoothing the top of the batter. Make a trench down the center of the batter using a spoon. Bake at 350 degrees for 55 minutes or until a wooden pick inserted in the center comes out clean, rotating the pans from front to back halfway through baking. Remove to a wire rack and place a damp paper towel on top of each loaf.

Cover the pans with foil and let the loaves cool. Remove the loaves from the pans. Wrap in plastic wrap and freeze for at least 3 hours. Remove the frozen loaves to a cutting board and remove the plastic wrap. Cut carefully with a serrated knife into $1/_4$-inch slices. Arrange on a cookie sheet. Bake at 325 degrees for 15 to 25 minutes or until dry and light brown, rotating the cookie sheet once or twice for even browning. Remove to a wire rack to cool. Store in an airtight container. **Makes 3 to 4 dozen biscotti.**

Note: You may use dried cranberries or dried cherries instead of crystallized ginger.

CHEWY CHOCOLATE CHIP OATMEAL COOKIES

2 cups all-purpose flour
1 teaspoon baking soda
1 teaspoon baking powder
1 teaspoon salt
1 cup (2 sticks) butter, softened
1 1/2 cups packed dark brown sugar

1 egg
1 tablespoon water
2 teaspoons vanilla extract
2 cups quick-cooking oats
1 cup (6 ounces) chocolate chips

Mix the flour, baking soda, baking powder and salt together. Beat the butter and brown sugar in a bowl until light and fluffy. Beat in the egg, water and vanilla. Add the dry ingredients and mix well. Stir in the oats. Stir in the chocolate chips. Drop by walnut-size spoonfuls onto a nonstick cookie sheet. Flatten the dough with your fingers or a fork.

Bake at 350 degrees for 10 minutes. Cool on the cookie sheet for 5 minutes. Remove to paper towels to cool. *Makes 4 dozen cookies.*

Note: You may add 1 cup dried cherries and/or 1 tablespoon grated orange zest, if desired.

CHOCOLATE TRUFFLE COOKIES

1/2 cup all-purpose flour
1/2 teaspoon baking powder
1/4 cup (1/2 stick) unsalted butter
1 cup (6 ounces) semisweet chocolate chips
4 ounces unsweetened chocolate
4 eggs

1 1/2 cups sugar
1 teaspoon vanilla extract
4 teaspoons freeze-dried coffee granules
4 1/2 cups ground walnuts
1 cup (6 ounces) semisweet chocolate chips

Mix the flour and baking powder together. Combine the butter and 1 cup chocolate chips in the top of a double boiler. Cook over simmering water until melted and smooth, stirring occasionally. Add the unsweetened chocolate. Cook until melted; do not stir. Remove from the heat. Combine the eggs, sugar, vanilla and coffee granules in a bowl and beat well.

Stir in the melted chocolate mixture gradually. Add the dry ingredients and mix well. Stir in the walnuts and 1 cup chocolate chips. Shape by teaspoonfuls into ovals on a greased cookie sheet. Bake at 350 degrees for 5 minutes or until the tops are slightly cracked. Cool on the cookie sheet for 5 minutes. Remove to a wire rack to cool completely. *Makes 5 to 6 dozen cookies.*

COCONUT MACAROONS

2 cups flaked coconut
1/2 cup sweetened condensed milk

Combine the coconut and sweetened condensed milk in a bowl and mix well. Drop by teaspoonfuls onto a nonstick cookie sheet and flatten slightly. Bake at 350 degrees for 8 to 9 minutes or until light brown.

Watch carefully so that the cookies do not get too brown. Cool on the cookie sheet for 5 minutes. Remove to a wire rack to cool completely. ***Makes 2 dozen cookies.***

FLOURLESS PEANUT BUTTER COOKIES

1 cup creamy or chunky peanut butter
1 cup (scant) sugar
1 egg, lightly beaten
1 teaspoon baking soda

Combine the peanut butter and sugar in a bowl. Beat with an electric mixer at medium speed for 2 minutes. Add the egg and baking soda and beat well. Shape by teaspoonfuls into balls. Place 1 inch apart on a lightly buttered cookie sheet. Flatten the cookies with a fork in a crisscross pattern to 1 1/2 inches in diameter.

Bake at 350 degrees on the middle oven rack for 10 minutes or until puffed and golden brown. Cool on the cookie sheet for 2 minutes. Remove to a wire rack to cool completely. Store the cookies in an airtight container or freeze. ***Makes 4 dozen cookies.***

FORGET 'EM MERINGUES

2 egg whites, at room temperature
¹/₈ teaspoon salt
³/₄ cup sugar
1 teaspoon vanilla extract
1 cup (6 ounces) chocolate chips
1 cup chopped pecans

Beat the egg whites in a bowl until foamy. Beat in the salt. Add the sugar 1 tablespoon at a time, beating constantly until stiff peaks form. Fold in the vanilla, chocolate chips and pecans. Drop by teaspoonfuls onto a foil-lined cookie sheet.

Place in a 350-degree oven. Turn off the oven. Leave in the oven for 8 hours without opening the oven door. Remove the cookies carefully from the foil. ***Makes 3 dozen cookies.***

SESAME COOKIES

1 cup (2 sticks) butter, softened
¹/₄ cup sugar
1 teaspoon almond extract
2 cups all-purpose flour
1¹/₂ teaspoons salt
Sesame seeds
Favorite fruit preserves

Beat the butter, sugar and almond extract in a bowl until light and fluffy. Add the flour and salt and beat well. Shape by spoonfuls into balls and roll in sesame seeds. Place the balls on a nonstick cookie sheet and flatten slightly, making an indentation in each ball.

Spoon a small amount of preserves into each indentation. Bake at 400 degrees for 10 to 12 minutes. Cool on the cookie sheet for 5 minutes. Remove to a wire rack to cool completely. ***Makes 4 dozen cookies.***

ALMOND COCONUT FUDGE SUNDAE TOPPING

¹/2 cup (1 stick) unsalted butter
2 (4-ounce) packages sliced almonds
1¹/2 cups flaked coconut
²/3 cup heavy cream
2 cups (12 ounces) semisweet chocolate chips
2 teaspoons vanilla extract

Melt the butter in a heavy skillet. Add the almonds and coconut and sauté until light brown. Remove to paper towels to drain. Combine the cream and chocolate chips in a 2-quart saucepan.

Cook over low heat until the chocolate is melted, stirring occasionally. Stir in the vanilla. Serve warm over ice cream and top with the coconut mixture. *Serves 8.*

WARM BLUEBERRY SAUCE

1¹/2 cups fresh blueberries
¹/4 cup sugar
³/4 teaspoon ground cinnamon
¹/4 teaspoon nutmeg
¹/2 teaspoon grated lemon zest

Combine the blueberries, sugar, cinnamon, nutmeg and lemon zest in a saucepan. Bring to a boil over medium heat, stirring occasionally. Reduce the heat.

Simmer for 5 minutes, stirring occasionally. Serve warm over vanilla ice cream. *Serves 4 to 6.*

SALTED CREAMY CARAMEL SAUCE

1³/₄ cups sugar
¹/₂ cup corn syrup
2¹/₄ cups hot heavy cream
2 teaspoons kosher salt

Combine the sugar and corn syrup in a deep saucepan. Cook over medium heat to a deep amber color, stirring occasionally. Pour in the hot cream slowly and carefully, stirring constantly. Stir in the salt.

Cook until the salt is dissolved, stirring constantly. Strain through a mesh strainer into a bowl. Season with additional salt, if desired. Serve over ice cream and fresh fruit. *Serves 16.*

A PITCHER OF HUMMERS

A favorite recipe from a past president

³/₄ cup Kahlúa
¹/₂ cup light rum
¹/₄ cup crème de cacao
¹/₂ gallon vanilla ice cream

Combine the Kahlúa, rum, crème de cacao and half the ice cream in a blender and process until smooth. Add the remaining ice cream and process until smooth.

Pour into glasses and serve, or pour into an ice bucket and freeze until ready to serve. Stir before spooning into glasses. *Serves 10.*

Note: You may omit the crème de cacao and increase the light rum to ³/₄ cup.

MOCHA COFFEE

5 tablespoons baking cocoa
5 tablespoons sugar
$1/2$ cup cold water
Pinch of salt
1 cup boiling water
$1^1/2$ cups strong coffee
$1^1/2$ cups evaporated milk
Kahlúa (optional)

Combine the baking cocoa, sugar, cold water and salt in a saucepan. Cook over low heat for 2 to 3 minutes, stirring constantly. Stir in the boiling water, coffee and evaporated milk.

Bring to a boil. Remove from the heat and beat until frothy. Pour into cups and serve with the Kahlúa.
Serves 5 or 6.

For a smooth and delicious after-dinner drink, mix equal amounts of amaretto and Irish cream. Add vodka if a less sweet mixture is desired. Serve over ice.

RECID CONTRIBUTORS

In commemoration of our 50th year, The Village Club presents its third cookbook, *Popovers to Panache: Food with a Flair from The Village Club*. It is full of prized recipes from Village Club members, and we hope that in years to come it will display turned down corners, notes on the pages, a few spills on favorite recipes, and all in all . . . will have been well used.

In celebration of The Village Club's 50th anniversary our members submitted their best recipes to share with you. Every recipe has been thoroughly tested. We revised and retested until we "got it right." The Cookbook Development Committee is deeply grateful to all who shared their culinary knowledge and favorite recipes, and thank you sincerely for your contribution. We apologize if we have overlooked anyone.

Sharon Adams	Patricia Ciagne	Liz Galbraith	Emily Karalash
Diana Aginian	Phyllis N. Clark	Lois Gamble	Barbara L. Keller
Margie Allen	Eunice Coffman	Judy Gardner	Kathleen Kennedy
Edie Anderson	Martha Condit	Tolly Gaul	Sally Kerr
Sue Andrews	Freddie Corrigan	Gail Geiger	Nancy Kleckner
Molly Appleford	Ann Corwell	Kate Gladchun	Betty Kneen
Dorothy Arcari	Jane Dallas	Dorothy W. Goodwin	Sue Knisley
Jean Auchterlonie	Judith Darin	Mary Ann Greenawalt	Anne Koprince
Barbara Ballantyne	Peg Dasovic	Mary Lee Gwizdala	Chris Lamarche
Marlynn Barnes	Karen DeKoker	Jeanne Hackett	Jeanne Latcham
Wendy Beck	Connie Dugger	Juanita J. Hamel	Carol Lay
Martha Beechler	Barbara Dundon	Peg Harber	Bobbi Long
Molly Beresford	Norma Dye	Pat Hardy	Marilyn "Garry" LoPrete
Pamela Bonk	Sandy Ebling	Judy Harris	Mary Lou Mabee
Frances Booth	Dorothy Ellis	Pat Haupt	Suzanne MacDonald
Joan Bowes	Janette Englehardt	Christina Heidrich	Donna M. MacInnes
Camille Breen	Anne Farnen	Brenda Hile	Sandy Mackle
Tenney Brinkman	Margie Fitts	Sandy Hufnagle	Rebecca Magnus
Margaret Brophy	Mickie Frederick	June Wilsey Hullinger	Martha Maxwell
Mary Callam	Lois F. Fredericks	Marion M. Hyde	Phyllis Mazure
Loris Caplan	Elaine Freidinger	Sally Ingold	Barbara McCuiston
Barbara Caponigro	Sharon Frost	Dorothy "Dolly" Johnson	
Sharrie Cheff	Sandy Futterknecht	Virginia Johnston	*continued on next page*

RECIPE CONTRIBUTORS

Patty McGillivray

Denise McKewan

Becky McLennan

Barbara Meach

Lillian Mitchell

Dede Moody

Del Moore

Linda Morrow

Chuck Murray

Nancy Murray

Martha Neumann

Cecily O'Connor

Joyce Oldham

Jackie Ong

Amy Palmer

Sally Parsons

Nancy Peil

Barbara Peirce

Helen Peterson

Wendy Petherick

Mitzi Phillips

Cathie Pollock

Sarah Post

Mary Louise Pridmore

Lynn Quigley

Barbara Quinn

Eunice Raar

Marjorie A. Rader

Kirsteen Reeve

Maurcina Reuss

Joyce Rolf

Mary Ann Rosenberger

Kathleen Royer

Barbara Russell

Connie Salloum

Ruth Sanders

Annette Saylor

Jean Schuler

Nancy Schutte

Trudy Schwarz

Kathy Shaieb

Louise Simpson

Mary Smart

Marilyn "Jigger" Smith

Patricia Smith

Nancy Spence

Margie Stoller

Bernice Street

Karen Rickets Struck

Sally Struck

Jane S. Sullivan

Margaret A. Suter

Jan Swanson

Mary Tamsen

Patricia Tennent

Anita Terry

Rosalyn Huyette Thompson

Lois Thornbury

Martha Torre

Francie Utley

Elizabeth Van Vurst

Lorraine Walsh

Pat Wasson

Patricia Wenstrand

Joan West

Trudy White

Linda Wilson

Virgina S. Wilson

Marcia Wiltshire

Ava Wixted

Carol Worsley

Marion Wyatt

Helena Zabriskie

Barbara Zimmerman

Chef Chris Richter and
   The Village Club Kitchen Staff

INDEX

Accompaniments
Candied Walnuts, 18
Cantaloupe and Cherry Tomato
  Salsa, 132
Cranberry Conserve, 132
Pineapple Avocado Salsa, 133
Tomato Chutney, 129

Appetizers. *See also* Dips; Spreads
Apricot Coins, 18
Crab Meat and Shrimp
  Cocktail with Red
  Pepper Aïoli, 13
Lemon Parmesan Artichoke
  Bottoms, 15
Mushroom Roll-Ups, 16
Olive Paste and Blue Cheese
  Canapés, 16
Prosciutto and Ricotta Pita
  Pockets, 15
Snack-Style Shrimp, 14
Snow Peas Stuffed with Herb
  Cheese, 17
Walnut- and Cheese-Stuffed
  Cucumbers, 17

Apples
Apple and Nut Upside-Down
  Cake, 138
Apple-Topped Brie, 21
Spinach and Apple Salad, 54
Splendid Fruit Crisp, 149
Sweet-and-Sour Red Cabbage
  with Apples, 122
Tarte Tatin, 156

Artichokes
Artichoke and Spinach
  Casserole, 120
Cod with Tomato and Artichoke
  Sauce, 108
Crab and Artichoke
  Dip, 22
Lemon Parmesan Artichoke
  Bottoms, 15

Asparagus
Asparagus Frittata, 68

Savory Bread Pudding with
  Spring Herbs, 70
Vegetable Bisque, 42

Avocados
Avocado and Citrus Salad with
  Pomegranate Seeds, 49
California Salad with Lemon
  Mustard Dressing, 53
Condiment Chicken Salad, 59
Crab Meat and Shrimp Cocktail
  with Red Pepper Aïoli, 13
Pineapple Avocado Salsa, 133
Roquefort Pear Salad, 52

Bananas
Banana Date Nut Muffins, 73
Cake That Won't Last, 78

Beans
Black Bean Chicken Chili, 101
Garden Corn and Black Bean
  Salad, 58
Hearty Mexican Soup, 32
Marinated Green Beans with
  Red Onion, 121
Northern Bean Casserole, 121
Quick Summer Minestrone, 43
Quinoa and Black Bean
  Salad, 62
San Diego Tortilla Soup, 33
Senate Bean Soup, 33
Tuscan Vegetable Soup, 44
White Bean Dip, 25
White Chili, 101

Beef
Beef Brisket, 85
Boursin Leek Soup, 36
Dry Rub for Beef, Pork or
  Poultry Barbecue, 115
Monterey Lasagna, 87
Oven-Roasted Beef
  Tenderloin, 85
Reuben Cocktail Dip, 24
Roast Beef Tenderloin in a Dry
  Rub Crust, 86
Spaghetti Pie, 91

Berries. *See also* Blueberries;
  Raspberries
Chilled Hungarian Berry
  Soup, 45
Strawberry Pavlova, 148
Strawberry Salad with Poppy
  Seeds, 54

Beverages
A Pitcher of Hummers, 167
Brandy Slush, 25
Cosmopolitan Cocktail, 27
Mocha Coffee, 168
Pretty Peach Cocktail, 26

Biscotti
Pecan and Ginger Biscotti, 162
Triple-Chocolate Biscotti, 161

Blueberries
Blueberry Buckle, 80
Blueberry Pound Cake, 150
Chicken Blueberry
  Salad, 59
Lemon Blueberry Biscuits, 75
Summer Blueberry Raspberry
  Pie, 154
Warm Blueberry Sauce, 166

Breads. *See also* Coffee Cakes;
  Muffins; Pancakes
Buttermilk Date Orange
  Scones, 74
Gougère, 71
Lemon Blueberry Biscuits, 75
Lemon Bread, 71
Orange Bread, 71
Pumpkin Bread, 72
The Village Club
  Popovers, 74
Two Ways to Make French
  Toast, 76
Wheat Germ Zucchini
  Bread, 72

Broccoli
Broccoli Slaw, 56
Layered Broccoli Salad, 56

Brussels Sprouts
Brussels Sprouts and Cherry
  Tomato Salad, 57
Brussels Sprouts in Pecan
  Butter, 122

Cabbage
Cabbage Soup, 34
Sweet-and-Sour Red Cabbage
  with Apples, 122
Tuscan Vegetable Soup, 44

Cakes
Apple and Nut Upside-Down
  Cake, 138
Black Russian Cake, 150
Blueberry Pound Cake, 150
Cake That Won't Last, 78
Double-Chocolate Mousse
  Cake, 137
Getty Museum Carrot
  Cake, 151
Ginger Cake in a Blackened
  Skillet, 151
Luscious Lemon Cake, 152
Molten Chocolate Cakes, 138
Pumpkin Cake Roll, 153

Carrots
Carrot Dill Soup, 34
Crème des Carottes de
  Crécy, 35
Getty Museum Carrot
  Cake, 151
One-Dish Salmon, 109

Cauliflower
Cauliflower Purée in Tomato
  Cups, 123
Cauliflower Soup, 35
Mashed Cauliflower, 123

Cherries
Cherry Chicken Jubilee, 97
Cherry Oatmeal Muffins, 73
Dried Cherry and Toasted
  Pecan Salad with Maple
  Dressing, 51

INDEX

Chicken
Bengel Tigers, 97
Black Bean Chicken Chili, 101
Calypso Chicken, 100
Cherry Chicken Jubilee, 97
Chicken Blueberry Salad, 59
Chicken Soufflé, 69
Chicken Thighs Baked with
    Lemon, Sage, Rosemary and
    Thyme, 99
Chicken with Wild Rice
    Chowder, 32
Condiment Chicken Salad, 59
Hearty Mexican Soup, 32
Hot Chicken Salad, 100
Mexican Caesar Salad, 60
My Favorite Chicken
    Salad, 60
Oriental Mushroom Soup, 31
Quick-and-Easy Whiskey
    Chicken, 98
San Diego Tortilla Soup, 33
Winter Chicken, 98

Chilies
Black Bean Chicken Chili, 101
White Chili, 101

Chocolate
Almond Coconut Fudge
    Sundae Topping, 166
Black Russian Cake, 150
Chewy Chocolate Chip
    Oatmeal Cookies, 163
Chocolate Glaze, 137
Chocolate Mint Frosting, 159
Chocolate Truffle
    Cookies, 163
Double-Chocolate Mousse
    Cake, 137
Easy Oreo Ice Cream, 143
Forget 'em Meringues, 165
Good and Easy Brownies, 158
Grasshopper Bars, 159
Mocha Coffee, 168
Molten Chocolate
    Cakes, 138
Mousse in a Minute, 141

Sour Cream Orange Coffee
    Cake, 79
Triple-Chocolate Biscotti, 161
Unhumble Raspberry Chocolate
    Pie, 155

Coffee Cakes
Blueberry Buckle, 80
Cinnamon Pecan Coffee
    Cake, 78
Sour Cream Orange Coffee
    Cake, 79

Cookies. *See also* Biscotti
Breakfast Cookies, 81
Chewy Chocolate Chip
    Oatmeal Cookies, 163
Chocolate Truffle
    Cookies, 163
Coconut Macaroons, 164
Flourless Peanut Butter
    Cookies, 164
Forget 'em Meringues, 165
Sesame Cookies, 165

Cookies, Bar
Butter Tart Squares, 158
Good and Easy
    Brownies, 158
Grasshopper Bars, 159
Imperial Squares, 160
Inventory Bars, 160
Lemon Cornmeal Shortbread
    Bars, 161

Corn
Corn Casserole, 124
Farm Fresh Corn Salad, 57
Garden Corn and Black Bean
    Salad, 58

Crab Meat
Crab and Artichoke Dip, 22
Crab Cakes and Tartar
    Sauce, 104
Crab Meat and Shrimp
    Cocktail with Red Pepper
    Aïoli, 13

Cucumbers
Chilled Herbed Cucumber
    Soup, 45
Walnut- and Cheese-Stuffed
    Cucumbers, 17

Desserts. *See also* Cakes; Cookies;
    Pies; Puddings; Sauces,
    Dessert; Tarts
Baked Manchego Cheese with
    Pear Compote and Sliced
    Pears, 146
Blueberry Buckle, 80
Easy Oreo Ice Cream, 143
Fabulous Raspberry
    Cheesecake, 142
Fig Compote with Honey and
    Thyme, 145
Frozen Lemon Cream, 144
Fruit Salsa Sundaes, 149
Hollywood's Favorite
    Cheesecake, 143
Hot Curried Fruit, 80
Lemon Delicacy, 141
Mousse in a Minute, 141
Pears Poached in Spiced Red
    Wine, 147
Poached Pears with Cinnamon
    Ice Cream and Strawberry
    Raspberry Coulis, 147
Rhubarb Squares, 148
Splendid Fruit Crisp, 149
Strawberry Pavlova, 148
White Forest Torte, 142

Dips
Baked Vidalia Onion Dip, 23
Crab and Artichoke Dip, 22
Reuben Cocktail Dip, 24
Roasted Red Pepper Dip, 24
White Bean Dip, 25

Egg Dishes
Asparagus Frittata, 68
Cheese Soufflé, 68
Chicken Soufflé, 69
Chile Relleno
    Casserole, 69

Quick Quiche, 67
Savory Bread Pudding with
    Spring Herbs, 70
Spinach Quiche, 67

Eggplant
Crispy Eggplant, 125
Easy Ratatouille, 124

Fish. *See also* Salmon
Cod with Tomato and
    Artichoke Sauce, 108
Grilled Halibut, 104
Hoisin-Glazed Sea Bass, 113
Honey Soy Ahi Tuna
    Steaks, 113
Oriental Grouper, 108
Roasted Halibut with Fresh
    Herb Sauce, 105
Seafood Stew with Tomatoes,
    Shrimp and Scallops, 107
Smoked Trout and Shrimp
    Pâté, 19

Frostings/Glazes
Chocolate Glaze, 137
Chocolate Mint
    Frosting, 159
Lemon Glaze, 152

Fruit. *See also* Apples; Avocados;
    Bananas; Berries; Cherries;
    Peaches; Pears; Pineapple;
    Pumpkin
Fruit Salsa Sundaes, 149
Splendid Fruit Crisp, 149

Game
Cornish Hens with Winter
    Fruit, 103
Loin of Venison with Mustard
    Pepper Marinade, 96
Pheasant with Shotgun
    Sauce, 103

Grains. *See also* Rice
Cranberry Tabouli, 63
Granola, 81

INDEX

Mushroom Barley Soup, 36
Quinoa and Black Bean
  Salad, 62
Tabouli Salad, 63

Lamb
Braised Lamb Shanks, 94
Marinated Greek Butterflied
  Lamb, 94
Rosemary-Marinated Lamb on
  the Grill, 95
Tarragon Lemon Rack of
  Lamb, 95

Muffins
Banana Date Nut
  Muffins, 73
Cherry Oatmeal Muffins, 73

Mushrooms
Mushroom Barley Soup, 36
Mushroom Roll-Ups, 16
Oriental Mushroom
  Soup, 31
Stuffed Mushrooms, 125

Nuts
Candied Walnuts, 18

Pancakes
Deluxe Pancake Mix, 77
Favorite Pancake, 77

Pasta
Bow Tie Pasta with Fresh
  Tomato Basil Sauce, 114
Linguini with Shrimp and
  Sun-Dried Tomatoes, 106
Monterey Lasagna
  (non-pasta), 87
Penne with Sausage and
  Broccoli Rabe, 92
Spaghetti Pie, 91

Peaches
Golden Glow Pork
  Chops, 87
Hot Curried Fruit, 80

Pretty Peach Cocktail, 26
Splendid Fruit Crisp, 149

Pears
Baked Manchego Cheese
  with Pear Compote and
  Sliced Pears, 146
Hot Curried Fruit, 80
Pear Compote, 146
Pears Poached in Spiced Red
  Wine, 147
Poached Pears with Cinnamon
  Ice Cream and Strawberry
  Raspberry Coulis, 147
Roquefort Pear Salad, 52

Pies
Ice Cream Pie
  Spectacular, 144
Pecan Date Pie, 153
Praline Ice Cream Pie with
  Caramel Sauce, 145
Summer Blueberry Raspberry
  Pie, 154
Unhumble Raspberry Chocolate
  Pie, 155

Pineapple
Baked Pineapple, 133
Cake That Won't Last, 78
Getty Museum Carrot
  Cake, 151
Hot Curried Fruit, 80

Pizza
Tuscan Pizza, 93

Pork. *See also* Prosciutto; Sausage
Baked Pork Tenderloin with
  Mustard Sauce, 89
Curried Back of Pork
  Ribs, 90
Dry Rub for Beef, Pork or
  Poultry Barbecue, 115
Golden Glow Pork Chops, 87
Pork Loin Piccata, 89
Pork Tenderloin with Maple
  Mustard Sauce, 88

Potatoes. *See also* Sweet Potatoes
Cold Vegetables with Mustard
  Sauce, 131
Oven Potato Puff, 128
Scalloped Potatoes, 127
Zucchini Soup, 39

Poultry. *See also* Chicken; Turkey
Dry Rub for Beef, Pork or
  Poultry Barbecue, 115

Prosciutto
Fig and Prosciutto Salad, 49
Prosciutto and Ricotta Pita
  Pockets, 15

Puddings
Decadent Bread Pudding, 139
Holiday Cranberry Steamed
  Pudding, 139
Sticky Date Pudding with
  Caramel Sauce, 140

Pumpkin
Pumpkin Bread, 72
Pumpkin Cake Roll, 153

Raspberries
Fabulous Raspberry
  Cheesecake, 142
Fruit Salsa Sundaes, 149
Pretty Peach Cocktail, 26
Raspberry Orange Lettuce
  Salad, 50
Splendid Fruit Crisp, 149
Summer Blueberry Raspberry
  Pie, 154
Unhumble Raspberry Chocolate
  Pie, 155

Rice
Chicken with Wild Rice
  Chowder, 32
Creamy Lemon Rice, 120
Curried Back of Pork Ribs, 90
Smoked Sausage Gumbo, 91
Spinach Feta Rice, 119
Turkey Madras, 102

Salad Dressings
Lemon Mustard Dressing, 53
Maple Dressing, 51
Martha's Vineyard
  Dressing, 52
Mexican Caesar Dressing, 60
Raspberry Vinaigrette, 50

Salads
Avocado and Citrus Salad with
  Pomegranate Seeds, 49
Broccoli Slaw, 56
Brussels Sprouts and Cherry
  Tomato Salad, 57
California Salad with Lemon
  Mustard Dressing, 53
Chicken Blueberry Salad, 59
Cold Sweet Potato Salad, 58
Condiment Chicken
  Salad, 59
Cranberry Tabouli, 63
Dilled Shrimp and Feta Cheese
  Salad, 61
Dried Cherry and Toasted
  Pecan Salad with Maple
  Dressing, 51
Farm Fresh Corn Salad, 57
Fig and Prosciutto Salad, 49
Garden Corn and Black Bean
  Salad, 58
Layered Broccoli Salad, 56
Martha's Vineyard Salad, 52
Mexican Caesar Salad, 60
My Favorite Chicken
  Salad, 60
Quinoa and Black Bean
  Salad, 62
Raspberry Orange Lettuce
  Salad, 50
Roquefort Pear Salad, 52
Shrimp Salad with
  Romaine, 61
Spinach and Apple Salad, 54
Spinach Beet Salad with Roasted
  Shallot Dressing, 55
Strawberry Salad with Poppy
  Seeds, 54
Tabouli Salad, 63

INDEX

Salmon
Chilled Poached Salmon with
   Mustard Dill Sauce, 110
One-Dish Salmon, 109
Seared Roasted Salmon Fillets
   with Lemon Ginger Butter, 110
Smoked Salmon Spread, 19
Special Grilled Salmon, 111
Spiced Salmon with Yellow
   Peppers, 112

Sauces, Dessert
Almond Coconut Fudge
   Sundae Topping, 166
Caramel Sauce, 140
Salted Creamy Caramel
   Sauce, 167
Warm Blueberry Sauce, 166

Sauces, Savory
Fresh Herb Sauce, 105
Mustard Sauce, 89
Pesto, 22
Red Pepper Aïoli, 13
Sambuca Cream, 37
Tartar Sauce, 104
Wine Sauce, 86

Sausage
Penne with Sausage and
   Broccoli Rabe, 92
Smoked Sausage Gumbo, 91
Spaghetti Pie, 91
Spinach Quiche, 67
Tuscan Pizza, 93

Scallops
Garlicky Scallops and
   Shrimp, 106
Seafood Stew with Tomatoes,
   Shrimp and Scallops, 107

Seafood. *See* Crab Meat; Fish;
   Scallops; Shrimp

Shrimp
Crab Meat and Shrimp Cocktail
   with Red Pepper Aïoli, 13
Dilled Shrimp and Feta Cheese
   Salad, 61
Garlicky Scallops and
   Shrimp, 106
Linguini with Shrimp and
   Sun-Dried Tomatoes, 106
Seafood Stew with Tomatoes,
   Shrimp and Scallops, 107
Shrimp Salad with
   Romaine, 61
Smoked Trout and Shrimp
   Pâté, 19
Snack-Style Shrimp, 14

Side Dishes. *See also*
   Accompaniments; Rice;
   Vegetables
Baked Pineapple, 133
Blue Cheese Polenta, 119
Hot Curried Fruit, 80
Pear Compote, 146

Soups. *See also* Chilies
Boursin Leek Soup, 36
Cabbage Soup, 34
Carrot Dill Soup, 34
Cauliflower Soup, 35
Chicken with Wild Rice
   Chowder, 32
Chilled Herbed Cucumber
   Soup, 45
Chilled Hungarian Berry
   Soup, 45
Consommé, 41
Crème des Carottes
   de Crécy, 35
Curried Squash Soup, 40
Dynamite Vegetable
   Chowder, 43
Hearty Mexican Soup, 32
Mushroom Barley Soup, 36

Oriental Mushroom
   Soup, 31
Quick Summer
   Minestrone, 43
Red Pepper Soup with Sambuca
   Cream, 37
Roquefort and Spinach
   Soup, 38
San Diego Tortilla Soup, 33
Seafood Stew with Tomatoes,
   Shrimp and Scallops, 107
Senate Bean Soup, 33
Spinach Bisque, 37
Thai Coconut Squash
   Soup, 38
Tomato Basil Soup, 40
Tuscan Vegetable Soup, 44
Vegetable Bisque, 42
Zucchini Soup, 39

Spinach
Artichoke and Spinach
   Casserole, 120
Roquefort and Spinach
   Soup, 38
Spinach and Apple Salad, 54
Spinach Beet Salad with
   Roasted Shallot Dressing, 55
Spinach Bisque, 37
Spinach Feta Rice, 119
Spinach Quiche, 67

Spreads
Apple-Topped Brie, 21
Basil and Currant Spread, 20
Brie with Apricots and
   Pine Nuts, 21
Curried Mélange Cheese
   Spread, 20
Mediterranean Cheese
   Torte, 22
Smoked Salmon Spread, 19
Smoked Trout and Shrimp
   Pâté, 19

Squash
Butternut Squash with a Twist, 129
Curried Squash Soup, 40
Thai Coconut Squash Soup, 38
Zucchini and Summer Squash
   Gratin, 130

Sweet Potatoes
Cold Sweet Potato Salad, 58
Roasted Curried Sweet
   Potatoes, 128

Tarts
Tarte Tatin, 156
Torta di Lemone, 157

Turkey
Apple-Brined Turkey, 102
Turkey Madras, 102

Vegetables. *See also* Artichokes;
   Asparagus; Beans; Broccoli;
   Brussels Sprouts; Cabbage;
   Carrots; Cauliflower; Corn;
   Cucumbers; Eggplant;
   Mushrooms; Potatoes;
   Spinach; Squash; Zucchini
Cold Vegetables with Mustard
   Sauce, 131
Dynamite Vegetable Chowder, 43
Easy Ratatouille, 124
Onions with Currant, Port and
   Balsamic Glaze, 126
Spicy Pimentos, 126
Tuscan Vegetable Soup, 44
Vegetable Bisque, 42

Zucchini
Cold Vegetables with Mustard
   Sauce, 131
Wheat Germ Zucchini Bread, 72
Zucchini and Summer Squash
   Gratin, 130
Zucchini Soup, 39

Looking To Our Future

50th Anniversary

Celebrating Our Past

The Village Club

190 East Long Lake Road
Bloomfield Hills, Michigan 48304
Tel: 248-644-3450
Fax: 248-644-7308
www.thevillageclub.org

Photocopies will be accepted.

**Please Print Clearly
Mail or Fax Order Form to The Village Club**

Date _____ / _____ / _____

Print Purchaser Name _____

Street Address _____

City _____ State _____ Zip _____

Telephone _____ E-mail _____

Quantity	Description	Cost
_____	Individual cookbooks at $24.95	$_____
_____	Case of 10 cookbooks at $225.00	$_____
	Subtotal	$_____

Michigan residents add 6% sales tax $_____

[   ] I will pick up the cookbooks at the club. $_____0.00_____
      No shipping and handling charge.

[   ] Ship cookbooks: First book at $5.00; $_____
      $2.00 for each additional book to same address.

Amount Due $_____

Method of Payment [   ] Charge to VC Member Account
                            Account Number _____

                       [   ] Check payable to The Village Club
                            Check Number _____

Purchaser Signature _____